C000135897

20–Minute Italian

Your Traditional Favorites, Faster, Easier and with a Modern Twist

Andrea Soranidis

founder of The Petite Cook

PAGE STREET
PUBLISHING CO.

PAGE STREET
PUBLISHING CO.

Copyright © 2019 Andrea Soranidis

First published in 2019 by

Page Street Publishing Co.

27 Congress Street, Suite 105

Salem, MA 01970

www.pagestreetpublishing.com

All rights reserved. No part of this book may be reproduced or used, in any form or by any means, electronic or mechanical, without prior permission in writing from the publisher.

Distributed by Macmillan, sales in Canada by The Canadian Manda Group.

23   22   21   20   19   1   2   3   4   5

ISBN-13: 978-1-62414-843-9

ISBN-10: 1-62414-843-3

Library of Congress Control Number: 2019932492

Cover and book design by Ashley Tenn for Page Street Publishing Co.

Photography by Andrea Soranidis

Printed and bound in China

Page Street Publishing protects our planet by donating to nonprofits like The Trustees, which focuses on local land conservation.

To Valerio and Noah

You're the salt & pepper of my life—
without you, it would be tasteless.

Table of Contents

Exciting Fish & Seafood Mains in a Blink 93

Pulses & Grains Ready in Less than 20 Minutes 111

Speedy Nutritious Salads 129

Effortless Everyday Sides 151

Introduction

Welcome to *20-Minute Italian*. I'm so happy you have picked up this book! I really hope it will give you a burst of inspiration to get you cooking awesome, fun, delicious and most importantly, *fast* Italian meals for your family and friends.

I was born and raised in Sicily, but I fell in love with London and moved to the U.K. by myself at the age of eighteen. Fast forward to today, ten years later, I've started my own little family, and I now live between London and a small picturesque town in Germany. Life has never been busier or better than this!

I've spent most of the last decade traveling around the world, developing my taste and discovering new ingredients, cuisines and techniques. I launched my food blog The Petite Cook in 2014 as a way to chronicle my foodie adventures and experiments in the kitchen.

I used to spend hours, even days, researching, tasting and experimenting with new dishes in the kitchen. But when I became a mum I had to learn to balance family life with my work as a food writer and photographer. I soon found myself returning more and more to the familiar Italian cuisine I grew up with. But this time, I had a decade of cooking experience and I was facing the lack of time typical of a new mum with a full-time career.

I began remaking the fast, nutritious meals my mum would cook up for me when I was a kid. A busy, working single mum, she somehow always managed to whip up traditional Italian meals from scratch in an instant, using simple pantry ingredients and whatever she found at the farmers' market on her way home from work.

When I was just a little girl, I would spend my days watching her making up the most delicious dinners for us. I wasn't allowed to cook—and I still need to ask permission whenever I visit!—but I was always around the kitchen, prepping the veggies and looking up at Mum as she cooked up a storm. I've locked all my favorite childhood meals in my memory: if I close my eyes, the smell of tomato sauce, the aroma coming from the pots of fresh herbs under the window, the sound of my mum jiggling the pans on the stove, all jump back to my mind and warm my heart like a bowl of hot meatballs.

Re-creating her meals and coming up with easier, faster versions of classic Italian recipes gave me the confidence to experiment more and more. And I began thinking, "maybe these recipes can actually help others who have as little time as I do!" What started as a way to feed my family the delicious meals we loved as quickly as possible soon became this awesome cookbook, which will hopefully make your busy life easier!

No matter where I live, I am Italian at heart, and my foodie soul rejoices at the sight of a bowl of pasta, or ricotta gnocchi or seared tuna in pistachio crust. I could carry on for pages . . . *20-Minute Italian* is a celebration of all my favorites, from the simple, glorious meals I grew up with to the dishes I love making for my little family and my friends.

There is a good mix of quintessential, must-try traditional Italian recipes and some more modern takes on classic favorites, which I have respectfully adapted to make them faster, easier and with a little extra zing. In some recipes, I've substituted a more internationally available option in place of an ingredient that's difficult to find or use outside Italy, such as panko breadcrumbs instead of Italian breadcrumbs, because they're more widely available and deliver 100% great results and consistency no matter where you live.

A few other recipes are not traditional but are a fresh combination of a couple of classic Italian ingredients, such as Sautéed Purple Potatoes & Romanesco Broccoli (page 166) paired with a dreamy velvety Parmesan sauce that you will want to pour on just about everything. In other words, I added a bit of my personal creativity to these traditional recipes, which I hope will give you an extra reason to love this universally beloved cuisine as much as I do.

The 75 recipes in this book will show you just how much you can do in 20 minutes. Some of these recipes are so simple and quick you could make them blindfolded. Others are more refined and will take a little extra care, but I promise, they're all worth having a go! I also deliberately included loads of plant-based and gluten-free recipes, and even the non-vegetarian recipes can be easily adapted into meat-free versions, so everyone you love can enjoy eating Italian.

Cooking and sharing my childhood cuisine warms my soul in so many happy ways. So, I hope that this collection of my favorite meals will feed your family and will bring the same big smile to their faces that Italian food brings to mine!

Quick & Easy Antipasti for All Occasions

Antipasti (appetizers) are fundamental in Italian cooking.

In the busy Sicilian kitchens of my childhood, any festive occasion was a good excuse to showcase an array of quick, vibrant and colorful antipasti platters to tickle the appetite before dinner.

So, whether you're putting together a feast for a crowd, or simply having a neighbor over for dinner, I've got you covered with some tasty ideas based on the incredibly flavorful plates of antipasti I grew up with.

These dishes are perfect as starters for a made-to-impress dinner party or for a lovely *aperitivo* with friends. This Italian custom consists of a pre-dinner drink served with small appetizers and is meant to "open" the palate, giving you a chance to relax, nibble and chat while you wait for dinnertime.

Believe me, it was hard to choose just a few, but I've managed to put together my all-time favorite quick and easy Italian appetizer recipes. I'm sure you'll love these speedy antipasti as much as my family and I do.

Fresh Burrata Panzanella in Just 10 Minutes

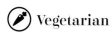 **Vegetarian**

A traditional Tuscan bread salad, panzanella is more than just a combination of tomatoes and stale bread. Ripe, in-season mixed tomatoes give an explosion of flavor when marinated with some good extra-virgin olive oil, toasted artisanal ciabatta bread and herbs. Top it off with a whole ball of cheesy, refreshing burrata and you've got a quick summer dish to feed a crowd with minimal effort.

Serves 4

½ clove garlic

3 thick slices artisanal ciabatta bread

5 tbsp (75 ml) fruity extra-virgin olive oil, divided

1 small red onion

½ large cucumber, seeds removed

12 oz (350 g) mixed tomatoes (heirloom, Pachino, Chocolate Sprinkles, Blondkopfchen, Piccadilly)

½ tbsp (1 g) freshly dried Italian oregano leaves

Sea salt and freshly cracked black pepper

Handful of basil leaves

9 oz (250 g) whole burrata cheese

Start by cutting the garlic in half lengthwise, then rub each side of the bread slices with the garlic clove. Cut the bread into ½- to ¾-inch (1- to 2-cm) cubes, and place them in a large bowl. Pour in 1 tablespoon (15 ml) of extra-virgin olive oil, and toss to combine. Heat a large grilling pan over medium heat, then add the bread cubes. Grill until nicely golden brown and crisp on each side, about 5 minutes. Remove and set aside to cool.

Finely slice the onion, finely chop the cucumber into small cubes and roughly chop all the tomatoes. Add all the ingredients to the same bowl used to season the bread cubes. Toss 4 tablespoons (60 ml) of extra-virgin olive oil and the oregano with the vegetables, and season the mixture with sea salt and black pepper to taste.

Fold the toasted bread cubes and basil leaves into the bowl, and stir to combine all the ingredients. Tear the burrata into small pieces and distribute over the panzanella.

Tip: *Find the best dried oregano you can. It's usually sold still in branches and is from Sicily. If you have trouble finding the burrata cheese, you can easily substitute buffalo or regular mozzarella cheese.*

Melon, Prosciutto & Mozzarella Skewers

 Gluten-Free

Melon and Parma prosciutto is a combo that screams Italian summer all the way! This super quick and incredibly easy evergreen appetizer features sweet, salty, gooey, crunchy, refreshing and aromatic notes all at once, which means every single bite is an explosion of flavor!

Serves 4

1 small cantaloupe

1 small honeydew melon

16 large basil leaves

8 slices Parma prosciutto

8 small mozzarella balls (*bocconcini*)

2 tbsp (30 ml) extra-virgin olive oil

Freshly cracked black pepper

Cut the cantaloupe and honeydew melons in half, scoop out all the seeds and discard them. Using a small melon baller, scoop out 8 balls from each melon.

Thread 1 cantaloupe ball onto a skewer, followed by a basil leaf, a slice of prosciutto, 1 mozzarella ball, another basil leaf and a honeydew melon ball. Repeat the process with the remaining skewers and ingredients.

Arrange the prepared skewers onto a serving plate and drizzle with the extra-virgin olive oil. Season with black pepper.

Tip: *For a more adventurous flavor, substitute the mozzarella with small chunks of hard cheese such as Pecorino or Parmesan.*

Beef Carpaccio & Asparagus Crostoni

Crostoni are similar to bruschetta; the only difference is that when it comes to crostoni, the bread is sliced very thinly. If you're not familiar with beef carpaccio, it's very thinly sliced raw meat, usually beef fillet or sirloin. Nowadays it is widely available at any Italian deli, or you can ask your local butcher to prepare it for you.

In this recipe, I've paired this delicate meat with deliciously crispy asparagus and crunchy crostoni to make a beautiful appetizer for an elegant dinner party. Did I mention it comes together in just about ten minutes? It's a win-win if you ask me!

Serves 4

8 medium-small asparagus

1 tbsp (15 ml) extra-virgin olive oil

Sea salt and freshly cracked black pepper

4 thin slices Italian ciabatta bread

¼ cup (60 g) fresh goat cheese

4 thin slices fresh beef carpaccio

1 tbsp (15 ml) fresh lemon juice

Bring a small pot of water to a boil.

Rinse the asparagus and pat them dry, then trim about ½ inch (1 cm) from their stalky ends. Place the asparagus into boiling water and cook for 5 minutes, or until just tender.

Drain the asparagus and pat them dry with paper towels.

Heat a small frying pan with the extra-virgin olive oil over medium heat. Add the asparagus and sauté them for 2 to 3 minutes. Season with sea salt and black pepper to taste, and transfer the asparagus to a plate.

Arrange the bread slices on the frying pan and toast them for 2 minutes on each side, until crispy and golden. Remove the bread slices from the pan and arrange them on a serving plate.

Spoon 1 tablespoon (15 g) of goat cheese onto each grilled bread slice and top with a slice of beef carpaccio and two asparagus. Drizzle the crostoni with the lemon juice.

Tip: *Goat cheese might have a strong flavor for some people, so you can substitute with ricotta cheese for a more delicate taste.*

Fresh Herb Frittata Sandwich Bites

🌾 Gluten-Free

Looking for a quick and tasty finger food idea for your next dinner party? I've got you covered! These deeply aromatic frittata sandwich bites feature all my favorite fresh herbs, packed in a spongy frittata with a creamy, slightly tangy lemon-and-ricotta filling.

Frittata is such an easy comforting dish, and with just a few clever touches, it can be easily transformed into a pretty finger food to entertain guests. I often prepare these frittata bites when I have friends over for dinner, and trust me, they disappear within seconds!

Serves 8

Small bunch of fresh parsley

Handful of fresh oregano

Handful of fresh mint

8 fresh large free-range eggs

3½ oz (100 g) freshly grated Grana Padano cheese

Sea salt and freshly cracked black pepper

2 tbsp (30 ml) extra-virgin olive oil

For the Ricotta Filling

3½ oz (100 g) fresh ricotta cheese, drained

1 tbsp (3 g) chopped chives

½ tsp fresh lemon zest

½ tsp extra-virgin olive oil

Sea salt and freshly cracked black pepper

Handful of fresh herbs, to decorate (optional)

Start by carefully washing all the herbs and drying them on paper towels. Gently pick off all the parsley, oregano and mint leaves, and discard the stems. Finely mince the leaves with a sharp knife, and set them aside.

In a medium-sized bowl, beat the eggs together with the Grana Padano cheese, and season with sea salt and black pepper. Fold in the chopped herbs, and beat until combined.

Heat a large pan over medium heat, and drizzle generously with the extra-virgin olive oil. Pour in the frittata mixture and cook for 2 minutes, gently shaking the pan every now and then.

When the frittata is easily pulled off from the bottom, it is ready to be turned. Using a plate the same diameter as the frittata, carefully put it on top of the pan and flip the frittata to the other side.

Return the frittata to the skillet, and cook uncovered for 5 minutes. Remove the skillet from the heat. Carefully slide the frittata onto a chopping board, slice it into 1-inch (2½-cm) cubes and allow them to cool for 5 minutes.

In the meantime, prepare the ricotta filling. In a small bowl, mix together the ricotta cheese with the chives, lemon zest and extra-virgin olive oil. Season with sea salt and black pepper to taste.

Place a teaspoon of ricotta mixture on top of a frittata cube, top with another frittata cube and gently secure with a toothpick. Top with extra ricotta mixture and decorate with fresh herbs (if using). Repeat the process with the remaining cubes, arrange them on a serving plate and serve at room temperature.

Tip: *Decorate the fresh herb frittata bites with fresh oregano, mint or basil leaves. You can also add them into the ricotta filling, if desired.*

Quick–Roasted Cherry Tomato & Ricotta Bruschetta

🥕 **Vegetarian**

Crunchy bread, sweet ricotta cheese and juicy pan-roasted tomatoes all come together for one of the best tomato bruschettas you can possibly eat.

Summertime is just the right season to enjoy this beautifully simple, flavor-packed bruschetta. I'm confident you'll agree that spending long hours in the kitchen when it's hot and sunny out there is not an option, so things like this bruschetta are just the perfect bite for a light lunch or an easy appetizer to share at dinner parties.

Serves 4

5 oz (150 g) cherry tomatoes on the vine (I recommend organic)

1 clove garlic, grated

2 sprigs of fresh thyme, leaves only

3 tbsp (45 ml) extra-virgin olive oil, divided

½ tsp high-quality balsamic vinegar

½ tsp fine brown sugar

Sea salt and freshly cracked black pepper

4 slices Italian rustic ciabatta bread

½ cup (120 g) fresh ricotta cheese

Optional Add–Ons

¼ cup (60 g) fresh Homemade Basil Pesto (page 35)

Handful of basil leaves

In a large bowl, combine the cherry tomatoes on the vine, garlic and thyme leaves. Drizzle with 2 tablespoons (30 ml) of extra-virgin olive oil and the balsamic vinegar, and sprinkle with the sugar. Season with sea salt and black pepper to taste, then toss gently to coat all the ingredients.

Heat a medium frying pan over medium heat. Add the tomatoes and their dressing. Cook for 3 minutes, then reduce the heat to low and cook for 10 minutes, gently shaking the pan every 2 to 3 minutes.

Heat a large grilling pan over medium heat. Brush the bread slices with the remaining 1 tablespoon (15 ml) of olive oil. Grill on both sides for 2 minutes, or until the bread is crispy and golden brown on both sides. Remove the bread slices from the pan, and arrange them on a serving plate.

Spoon 1 tablespoon (15 g) of ricotta cheese on each grilled bread slice, and top with a spoonful of pan-roasted tomatoes. Drizzle with basil pesto and/or decorate with basil leaves, if you like.

Easy Pappa al Pomodoro (Tuscan Tomato Soup)

🎁 Vegan

This traditional rustic Tuscan recipe is a comforting meal that requires simple, inexpensive Italian staple ingredients.

Ripe, juicy organic tomatoes are my go-to choice when they are in season, but to make this hearty, delicious soup all year round, go for canned Italian San Marzano peeled tomatoes. They're deeply sweet and loaded with flavor—an equally tasty and easy alternative to fresh tomatoes.

Serves 4

4 cups (1 L) vegetable stock, warm

2 tbsp (30 ml) extra-virgin olive oil, plus more for serving

1 clove garlic

1 lb (450 g) canned San Marzano tomatoes, undrained

Handful of basil leaves, divided

A pinch of brown sugar

Sea salt and freshly cracked black pepper

10½ oz (300 g) stale artisanal ciabatta bread, cut into chunks

Place the vegetable stock in a pot over low heat to keep it warm. Heat the extra-virgin olive oil in a large pan over medium heat. Add the garlic and cook for 30 seconds. Stir in the tomatoes and their juices, a couple of basil leaves and the pinch of sugar. Break the tomatoes into pieces, and season with sea salt and black pepper to taste. Cook, covered with a lid, over medium-low heat for about 10 minutes.

Place the bread into a large bowl, pour in the warm stock and let it sit undisturbed for 2 to 4 minutes. Transfer the bread to the pan with the tomato sauce, and stir constantly until the bread is fully incorporated into the sauce. Season with sea salt and black pepper to taste, scatter the remaining basil leaves over the top, drizzle with olive oil if desired and serve warm.

5-Minute Sicilian-Style Antipasto Platter

This is my go-to quick antipasti platter whenever I have friends over for drinks, or I'm simply enjoying a good glass of Nero d'Avola wine—a red Sicilian wine you definitely need to try!—with my other half. It's a fuss-free platter made with simple ingredients that remind me of my beautiful home. Making the best Sicilian-style platter comes down to just one thing: choosing the right ingredients. Sant'Angelo salami is a particular variety of salami made in Sicily; if you can't find it at your local Italian deli, swap it with the Neapolitan salami variety. Bright-green Castelvetrano olives are hugely popular outside of Sicily and for good reason—they're chunky, tender, mild in flavor and simply melt in your mouth. Last but not least, Bronte pistachios are sublimely sweet, moist and rich in flavor. They were even dubbed Sicily's "emerald green gem" by the *New York Times*!

These are just a few of my favorite ingredients. If you have a little more time, I recommend adding some tuna spread with crudites (page 32) and a few Eggplant, Ricotta & Fresh Herb Rolls (page 31) for the ultimate Sicilian-style antipasti platter!

Serves 4

8 slices Sant'Angelo salami

8 slices Parma prosciutto

8 small mozzarella balls (*bocconcini*)

3½ oz (100 g) Castelvetrano olives

3½ oz (100 g) caper berries

3½ oz (100 g) sun-dried tomatoes

3½ oz (100 g) spicy provolone, cubed

3½ oz (100 g) almonds, toasted

3½ oz (100 g) Bronte pistachios, toasted

8 artisanal breadsticks

8 rustic bread slices, toasted

Arrange the salami and prosciutto slices on a large serving board. Place the mozzarella balls, olives and caper berries in small bowls, and arrange them on the board.

Arrange the sun-dried tomatoes, provolone cheese, almonds, pistachios, breadsticks and bread slices on the board, filling any gaps. Serve along with your favorite drinks.

Poached Eggs in Italian-Style Tomato Sauce (Eggs in Purgatory)

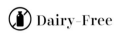 Dairy-Free

A simple spicy tomato sauce, organic eggs baked to perfection and crusty grilled bread to soak up all the flavorful sauce—this is the kind of meal I could have every day! What I love the most about this speedy classic Italian dish is that it can be easily whipped up with basic pantry staples. It makes a fantastic brunch or appetizer option, but it's also an awesome idea for a quick nutritious lunch.

Serves 4

3 tbsp (45 ml) extra-virgin olive oil, divided

1 clove garlic

½ tsp dried red chili pepper flakes

2 (28-oz [800-g]) cans whole plum tomatoes (I recommend organic), undrained

2 sprigs of fresh thyme

5 hand-torn basil leaves, divided

1 tsp freshly dried oregano leaves

A pinch of brown sugar

4 large eggs (I recommend organic)

Sea salt and freshly cracked black pepper

4 slices rustic bread

Heat 2 tablespoons (30 ml) of olive oil in a large frying pan over medium heat. Add the garlic and red chili pepper flakes and cook for 30 seconds. Stir in the tomatoes and their juices, the sprigs of thyme, a couple of basil leaves, the oregano and the pinch of sugar. Break the tomatoes into pieces with a wooden spoon and cook, letting the sauce bubble, for about 13 to 15 minutes over medium-low heat.

Use a spoon to make 4 small wells in the tomato sauce and crack an egg into each well. Season the eggs with sea salt and black pepper to taste. Cover the pan with a lid, and continue to cook over medium-low heat until the eggs are set, about 2 to 3 minutes for soft runny yolks.

While the eggs cook, heat a large grilling pan over medium-high heat and brush the bread slices with the remaining extra-virgin olive oil. Grill the bread until crispy on both sides, about 2 minutes.

Remove the eggs in purgatory from the heat. Sprinkle the remaining basil leaves on top, season with extra black pepper if desired and serve with the grilled bread.

Creamy Pumpkin Soup with Fried Sage & Amaretti

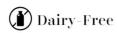 **Dairy-Free**

On cooler days, there's nothing better than digging into a big bowl of this comforting soup. Pumpkin and amaretti cookies may seem like an unusual combo, but they go beautifully together!

In Italy, these two ingredients are traditionally combined to make delicious filled pastas such as ravioli or tortelloni. Being a busy mum, I often find myself craving the flavor of those pumpkin ravioli, but I rarely have time to make filled pasta, and I rely on this soup to satisfy my craving. And boy it delivers! Sweet and aromatic, with a refreshing twist courtesy of the fried sage, this pumpkin soup is an absolute keeper.

Serves 4

For the Soup

2 tbsp (30 ml) extra-virgin olive oil

1 medium yellow or white onion, chopped

2 lb (900 g) pumpkin flesh, finely cubed

1 medium potato, peeled and finely cubed

1 tsp fresh thyme leaves

Sea salt and freshly cracked black pepper

4 cups (1 L) vegetable stock

½ tsp freshly grated nutmeg

¾ cup (60 g) amaretti cookies, crumbled, for serving

For the Fried Sage Leaves

¼ cup (60 ml) extra-virgin olive oil

Handful of fresh sage leaves

Sea salt flakes or fleur de sel

Heat the extra-virgin olive oil in a large pot over medium-high heat. Add in the onion, pumpkin and potato, followed by the thyme leaves. Sauté the ingredients for 5 minutes or until the vegetables begin to soften, then season with sea salt and black pepper to taste.

Pour in the stock and sprinkle with the nutmeg. Cover the pot with a lid and simmer for 10 to 15 minutes, or until the vegetables are cooked through.

Heat ¼ cup (60 ml) of olive oil in a small frying pan over medium heat. Add in 6 to 8 sage leaves at a time in a single layer and fry them until crispy and bright-green, about 2 to 3 seconds. Remove the sage leaves with a fork. Arrange them in a single layer on a plate covered with paper towels, then season with a pinch of sea salt flakes.

Remove the pot from the heat, and take 1 cup (240 ml) of stock out of the pot. Transfer the soup to a blender or use an immersion blender to blitz all the ingredients until it reaches your desired consistency, adding the reserved stock if necessary.

Divide the pumpkin soup among four bowls and sprinkle with the crumbled amaretti cookies. Decorate with the fried sage leaves and serve immediately.

Creamy Potato & Saffron Soup

  Gluten-Free, Vegan

Beautifully simple ingredients combine to make this elegant and surprisingly quick soup, with the saffron bringing it from standard to chic in a blink. I have deliberately decided to keep this soup as basic as possible, so you can easily customize it to meet your taste. If you like a little bit of heat, add a generous pinch of chili flakes, and for a bold kick of flavor, top with crispy pancetta.

Serves 4

2 tbsp (30 ml) extra-virgin olive oil, plus more for serving

1 medium yellow or white onion, chopped

2 lb (900 g) potatoes, peeled and finely cubed

1 tsp fresh thyme leaves

Sea salt and freshly cracked black pepper

4 cups (1 L) vegetable stock

A generous pinch of dried saffron

Heat the extra-virgin olive oil in a large pot over medium-high heat. Add in the onion and potatoes, followed by the thyme leaves. Sauté the ingredients for 5 minutes or until the vegetables begin to soften, then season with sea salt and black pepper to taste.

Pour in the stock, cover the pot with a lid and simmer for 10 to 15 minutes, or until the potatoes are tender.

Turn off the heat and stir in the saffron, then remove 1 cup (240 ml) of stock from the pot. Transfer the soup to a blender or use an immersion blender to blitz all the ingredients until it reaches your desired consistency, adding the reserved stock if necessary.

Divide the soup among four bowls, and drizzle with more extra-virgin olive oil. Sprinkle extra black pepper on top if desired, and serve immediately.

Eggplant, Ricotta & Fresh Herb Rolls

 Gluten-Free

This is my go-to appetizer for last-minute summer parties. The eggplant rolls feature a delicious combination of vibrant, aromatic herbs and creamy ricotta rolled up in slices of smoky grilled eggplant. I love to serve them as a finger food, or as part of my 5-Minute Sicilian-Style Antipasto Platter (page 23), but they also make a great side dish. I often pair them with a 10-Minute Mediterranean Couscous Salad (page 135) for a feel-good nourishing meal.

Serves 4

2 large dark-skinned Italian eggplants

3 tbsp + 1 tsp (45 ml + 5 ml) extra-virgin olive oil, divided

1 cup (240 g) ricotta cheese, drained

1 tbsp (2 g) fresh mint leaves, finely minced

1 tbsp (2 g) fresh basil leaves, finely minced

Zest of 1 lemon

3 tbsp (15 g) grated Parmesan cheese

2 tbsp (15 g) toasted pistachios, finely chopped

2 tbsp (30 g) fresh Homemade Basil Pesto (page 35)

Sea salt and freshly cracked black pepper

Cut off the edges of the eggplants and, with the help of a mandoline, slice them into thin ¼-inch (6-mm) slices. Brush both sides of each slice lightly with a total of 3 tablespoons (45 ml) extra-virgin olive oil.

Heat a nonstick grilling skillet over medium-high heat, add the eggplant slices in one layer and grill for 2 minutes on each side, or until golden brown on both sides. Remove the eggplant slices from the skillet, and repeat the process with the remaining slices.

In a small bowl, mix together the ricotta cheese with the remaining 1 teaspoon of extra-virgin olive oil, the fresh herbs, lemon zest, Parmesan cheese, pistachios and basil pesto. Season with sea salt and black pepper, and set aside.

Spread 1 heaping tablespoon (15 g) of the ricotta mixture onto a grilled eggplant slice and roll it up, then repeat the process with the remaining ingredients. Arrange the eggplant rolls on a serving plate and serve immediately.

Tips: *I like to add freshly made basil pesto (page 35) whenever I have it on hand. If you're short on time, feel free to leave it out.*

To make my life easier, I like to use a mandoline for this recipe. This super useful kitchen tool allows you to make thin, even slices in a fraction of the time. You can easily find one online and in most cookware stores.

5-Minute Salsa Tonnata (Tuna Spread) with Crudites

 Dairy-Free, Gluten-Free

Salsa tonnata translates to "tuna spread" or "tuna mayo." It is a super-traditional Italian recipe, usually served on top of thin slices of cooked veal at Christmas dinner parties. Salsa tonnata is loaded with flavor, and it comes together in a blink. So instead of serving it with slowly cooked meat, I find it perfect to liven up a plate of crudites, and I serve it all year long.

Serves 4

3½ oz (100 g) tuna fillets in a jar, drained

5 tbsp (45 g) capers, drained

1–2 anchovy fillets, drained

1 egg yolk, from a hard-boiled egg

½ cup (120 ml) extra-virgin olive oil

Zest and juice of ½ lemon

Sea salt

Vegetables of your choice, cut into sticks, for serving

Place the tuna fillets, capers, anchovy fillets and egg yolk in a food processor. Mix the ingredients on low speed, and slowly add the extra-virgin olive oil in a steady stream until fully incorporated with the other ingredients. Fold in the lemon zest and juice, and mix all ingredients until combined.

Season with sea salt to taste, and serve with fresh vegetables of your choice, cut into sticks.

Tip: *I like to serve my salsa tonnata with celery stalks, carrots and bell peppers, but feel free to use any veggies you like!*

Caprese Salad with Homemade Basil Pesto

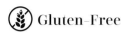 Gluten-Free

I'm one of those old-fashioned people who still loves to make traditional basil pesto by hand with the help of a mortar. I've tried the put-everything-in-a-mixer-and-blitz method and it just doesn't work out for me; the basil turns bitter and the ingredients just don't blend together as harmoniously as they are supposed to.

So, in an era where traditional recipes are getting lost, I wanted to share an evergreen recipe from my beloved Italian cuisine—and it really doesn't get "ever-greener" than classic basil pesto. Get a mortar—you can find one online and at most cookware stores—and try this recipe. It takes just ten minutes more than putting everything in a food processor, and I promise, you will never go back to store-bought pesto.

Use this pesto as your new go-to sauce to drizzle over a simple caprese salad as I did here, over grilled chicken or fish, and obviously as a quick sauce for a big bowl of pasta.

Serves 4

Homemade Basil Pesto

4 tbsp (30 g) pine nuts, toasted

½ clove garlic, finely minced

A pinch of kosher salt

8 cups (200 g) fresh basil leaves

⅔ cup (60 g) grated Parmesan cheese

3 tbsp (15 g) grated Pecorino Romano

½ cup (120 ml) extra-virgin olive oil

Caprese Salad

2 large mozzarella balls, drained and sliced

2 large tomatoes, sliced

Place the pine nuts, garlic and salt into a mortar. Crush them with the pestle until it reaches a paste-like consistency.

Gradually add in the basil leaves, crushing them with the pestle all the way through.

Crush all the ingredients until they turn into a creamy, bright-green paste.

Fold in the Parmesan cheese and Pecorino Romano, and mix all the ingredients until well combined.

Gradually add the extra-virgin olive oil in a thin, steady stream, until the pesto reaches a creamy consistency.

Arrange the mozzarella and the tomato slices, alternating them on a serving plate. Pour a couple of spoonfuls of the basil pesto over the mozzarella and tomato salad.

Tip: *This recipe makes about 3 cups (375 g) of basil pesto, so use any leftovers to dress a big bowl of pasta the next day!*

Cherry Tomatoes Stuffed with Herbs & Ricotta

  Gluten–Free, Vegetarian

Stuffing tomatoes is a fun way to serve them at summer parties and happy hours. There are tons of different fillings to choose from, but if I had to choose just one, I'd definitely pick this delicately aromatic ricotta cream made with fresh herbs and tangy lemon zest. It's super easy to prepare, and its refreshing flavor will leave you hungry for more.

Serves 4

12 cherry tomatoes (I recommend organic)

⅓ cup (85 g) fresh ricotta cheese, drained

1 tsp fresh basil leaves, finely chopped

1 tsp fresh thyme leaves

1 tsp fresh chives, finely chopped

1 tsp fresh mint leaves, finely chopped

Zest of ½ lemon

Sea salt and freshly cracked black pepper

Cut off the tops of the tomatoes and set them aside for decoration. Place the tomatoes top side down on a dish covered with paper towels for 5 minutes.

In a small bowl, mix together the ricotta with the herbs and lemon zest. Season with sea salt and black pepper to taste.

Transfer the ricotta mixture into a piping bag and fill each tomato with the mixture. Then add the reserved tomato tops over the ricotta mixture. Refrigerate the tomatoes for 5 minutes, then serve.

Tip: *Make sure to pick organic cherry tomatoes when they're in season. They're juicy, sweet and packed with flavor.*

Easy Pillowy Ricotta Gnocchi

Ricotta gnocchi are basically potato gnocchi's lighter, easier-to-make cousins—which is exactly why you should make them immediately! They're pretty easy and fun to pull together; ask your family or friends to help you out and you can make a big batch in less than fifteen minutes. These gnocchi have a lovely delicate flavor, so I like to serve them with a super quick brown butter & sage sauce, but a simple tomato sauce or my Homemade Basil Pesto (page 35) work really well too!

Serves 4

For the Gnocchi

17 oz (500 g) fresh whole-milk ricotta cheese, well drained

1 large egg (I recommend organic)

6 tbsp (30 g) grated Parmesan cheese

7 oz (200 g) all-purpose flour, divided (I recommend organic)

Sea salt

For the Sauce

3 tbsp (45 g) good-quality butter (I recommend organic)

10 small sage leaves

6 tbsp (30 g) grated Parmesan cheese

Freshly cracked black pepper

In a large bowl, stir together the ricotta, egg and Parmesan cheese until combined. Add three-quarters (150 g) of the flour and a generous pinch of salt. Work the dough with your hands until all the ingredients are incorporated.

Bring a large pot of water to a soft boil.

Sprinkle your hands and work surface with the remaining flour. Transfer the dough onto the surface, then gather it into a ball. It should have a soft but elastic texture; if it's too sticky, sprinkle in a little more flour. Flatten the ball into a large disk about 1 inch (2½ cm) thick. Cut the dough into ¾-inch (2-cm)-thick strips, then gently roll a strip into a rope about ¾ inch (2 cm) thick. Using a sharp knife, cut the rope crosswise every ¾ inch (2 cm) to make small logs. Arrange them on a baking tray covered with parchment paper, and repeat the process until all the dough has been used up.

Heat the butter in a large frying pan over low heat. Add the sage leaves and cook until the leaves are crispy, about 2 minutes.

Place the gnocchi into the soft-boiling water and simmer for 2 minutes. Remove ¼ cup (60 ml) of gnocchi cooking water from the pot and set it aside. Then drain the gnocchi and add them to the pan with the butter-sage sauce. Sprinkle the Parmesan cheese on top of the gnocchi, and stir all the ingredients together, adding a bit of gnocchi cooking water if necessary. Top the gnocchi with black pepper and serve immediately.

Tip: *Gnocchi freeze well and make an ideal last-minute meal. Spread uncooked gnocchi on a lightly floured sheet pan. Place them in the freezer until they are firm, about 30 minutes, then transfer them to a freezer bag and freeze for up to 1 month. Frozen gnocchi can be dropped directly into hot boiling water. Cook them for approximately 3 to 4 minutes or until just tender.*

Flashy Pasta & Risotto Dishes to Make on Repeat

Pasta is inexpensive, quick to prepare and makes dinner parties a breeze, because it allows you to improvise a whole meal to feed a crowd in just a few minutes. In Italy, it's common to receive impromptu, last-minute invitations from friends, and dinner will almost always involve a simple pasta such as Easy Spaghetti alla Carrettiera (page 64). The same applies to risotto, which can become an easy-to-make but elegant-looking entree for your next dinner party. With a minimal investment of time and money, you can make your family or friends happy and their bellies full.

You can't possibly get tired of pasta or risotto, because there are infinite ways to serve them, and they can be paired with an endless number of ingredients. Seafood, vegetables and meat all go amazingly with both pasta and risotto—but never, ever, add chicken, or else you'll lose the Italian friend you were looking forward to impressing with a lovely traditional meal! In fact, there's an unwritten rule in Italian cuisine to never pair pasta or risotto with chicken. It's hard to find a good explanation for this, but I can tell you this unusual combo makes Italians amusingly angry!

Most of the recipes you'll find here are really easy to customize. If you don't have an ingredient, try to substitute it with a similar one, or browse the other recipes to find a little more inspiration.

Finally, I'm very picky when it comes to pasta shapes, so I make my dishes with specific noodles. For example, I make my Creamy Pumpkin & Smoked Pancetta Pasta (page 59) only with paccheri or a very close shape (calamarata for instance)—but don't let my Italianess get in the way! Most of these recipes will work wonderfully with any shape of pasta you have. And remember, no matter what kind you choose, always cook it al dente!

Sicilian Pasta alla Norma

This is the queen of all Sicilian recipes, beloved by grown-ups and kids alike. According to the legend, this pasta recipe was SO good, it deserved to be named for the opera *Norma* by the great Italian compositor Vincenzo Bellini.

Tomatoes, eggplant, basil and *ricotta salata*—which translates to "salty aged ricotta," normally available online or at any Italian deli or large stores—are the few simple and inexpensive ingredients you need to make the classic Norma. It's a super easy and satisfying meal, perfect for busy weekdays or to please a large and hungry crowd.

Serves 4

1 large eggplant

1 cup + 1 tbsp (240 ml + 15 ml) extra-virgin olive oil, divided

5 whole canned plum tomatoes

1 clove garlic

½ cup (120 ml) warm water

4 basil leaves, divided

A pinch of brown sugar

Sea salt and freshly cracked black pepper

12 oz (350 g) spaghetti or short pasta, such as penne

3 tbsp (45 g) grated ricotta salata cheese

Bring a large pot of water to a boil.

Finely cube the eggplant, and pat the cubes dry with paper towels.

Heat 1 cup (240 ml) of extra-virgin olive oil in a large pan over medium heat. Add the eggplant in a single layer, and fry it until it's crispy and golden on both sides, about 4 minutes in total. Remove the eggplant with a slotted spoon and arrange the cubes in a single layer on a dish covered with paper towels. Dab the cubes with a paper towel to absorb the excess oil.

Slice the tomatoes in half, and remove the seeds. Heat a large pan with the remaining 1 tablespoon (15 ml) of extra-virgin olive oil and the garlic over medium heat. Fold in the tomatoes and stir-fry them for 5 minutes. Stir in the warm water, 2 basil leaves and the pinch of sugar, cover with a lid and cook for 10 to 15 minutes. Discard the garlic, and season the sauce with sea salt and black pepper to taste.

Lightly salt the boiling water, and add the pasta. Cook until al dente, according to package directions, about 8 minutes. Drain the pasta. Add it to the pan with the tomato sauce, followed by the fried eggplant cubes and the remaining basil leaves.

Stir all the ingredients together and sprinkle the ricotta salata all over the pasta.

Tip: *If you can't find ricotta salata, substitute with classic Parmesan cheese.*

Spicy Shrimp & Zucchini Linguine

🍶 **Dairy-Free**

This is a super easy pasta dish my mum loves to make on Sundays, whenever she finds fresh local shrimp at the market. It's a quick pasta that makes the most of crunchy zucchini and juicy, succulent, fresh shrimp. There are a lot of flavors going on already, but if you ask me, a pinch of dried chili flakes brings this dish to a whole new level.

Note: Just add a tiny pinch; my mum always adds too much. Mum, if you're reading, please use dried chili flakes responsibly.

Serves 4

12 oz (350 g) linguine pasta

2 zucchini

3 tbsp (45 ml) extra-virgin olive oil

½ clove garlic

A pinch of dried chili flakes

8 large shrimp, cleaned

Sea salt and freshly cracked black pepper

4–5 basil leaves, finely chopped

Bring a large pot of water to a boil. Lightly salt the boiling water and add the pasta. Cook until al dente, according to package directions, about 8 minutes.

Cut the zucchini in half, remove the seeds, chop them into very small cubes and pat them dry with paper towels.

Heat the extra-virgin olive oil in a large pan over medium heat. Add the zucchini cubes in a single layer and fry them until slightly crispy, about 4 minutes.

Add the garlic, chili flakes and shrimp, and cook all the ingredients for 2 minutes, or until the shrimp turn pink and are cooked through. Season with sea salt and black pepper to taste, then remove half of the shrimp, chop them roughly and return them to the pan.

Drain the pasta and add it into the pan with the zucchini and shrimp.

Stir all the ingredients together, and sprinkle the basil leaves all over the pasta.

Tip: *You can also replace basil leaves with mint leaves for a vibrant twist, and add a bit of lemon zest for a refreshing note.*

7-Ingredient Broccoli Pesto Pasta

(icon) Vegan

I have been serving this broccoli pesto for years, and my family still gets super excited whenever it's on the table. My other half has never been much of a broccoli fan, but he can easily devour a bowl of this pasta within seconds.

The flavor-packed broccoli pesto sauce beautifully embraces the orecchiette pasta—but you can choose any kind of pasta you like. The lemon zest gives a delightful refreshing twist, and the toasted pine nuts add a tiny bit of always-welcome crunch. Creamy, vibrant, loaded with nutritious goodness and awesomely vegan, this broccoli pesto pasta really has all it takes to make the broccoli-haters in your life change their mind.

Serves 4

12 oz (350 g) broccoli florets, halved

12 oz (350 g) orecchiette or other short pasta shape

Handful of fresh basil leaves

½ cup (60 g) toasted pine nuts

1 clove garlic, grated

Zest and juice of 1 lemon

¼ cup (60 ml) extra-virgin olive oil

Sea salt and freshly cracked black pepper

To Serve

2 tbsp (15 g) toasted pine nuts

Zest of ½ lemon

Handful of fresh basil leaves

Freshly cracked black pepper

Bring a large pot of lightly salted water to a boil, and as soon as the water boils, add the broccoli florets and cook for 4 to 5 minutes, or until tender.

With the help of a slotted spoon, transfer the florets from the water to a bowl with cold water and ice, then drain and set aside.

Add the pasta to the pot used for cooking the broccoli and cook until al dente, about 7 to 8 minutes for orecchiette. While the pasta is still cooking, remove ¼ cup (60 ml) of the water from the pot, and set it aside.

Place the broccoli florets, basil leaves, pine nuts, garlic, lemon juice and zest into a food processor. Pulse until it reaches a chunky consistency.

Set the food processor on slow speed and gently pour in the extra-virgin olive oil, then continue to mix on medium-high speed for about 2 minutes, or until the broccoli pesto reaches a creamy and dense texture.

Pour the reserved cooking water into the broccoli pesto, and continue to mix until it reaches the desired consistency. Season with sea salt and black pepper to taste.

Remove the pot from the heat, and drain the pasta. Return the pasta to the pot, stir in the broccoli pesto, and toss gently to combine all the ingredients.

Serve immediately with extra pine nuts, lemon zest, basil leaves and black pepper on top.

Tip: *To make a more traditional pesto sauce, double the amount of basil leaves and add in 6 tablespoons (30 g) of grated Parmesan cheese or Pecorino Romano.*

Smoked Salmon & Spinach Spaghetti

I make this for my family regularly because it's loaded with nutrient-packed ingredients, involves minimum preparation and has the most amazingly easy cream sauce made with fresh, light ricotta cheese. If you are a busy mum like me, this pasta is a total lifesaver. It's ready in just about fifteen minutes, making it the perfect option for a quick and healthy weeknight meal.

Serves 4

12 oz (350 g) spaghetti

2 tbsp (30 ml) extra-virgin olive oil, divided

1 small onion, finely chopped

4 oz (120 g) fresh baby spinach leaves

A pinch of nutmeg

Sea salt and freshly cracked black pepper

3½ oz (100 g) ricotta cheese

6 tbsp (30 g) grated Parmesan cheese

5 oz (150 g) smoked salmon, roughly chopped

½ tbsp (7 g) lemon zest

Bring a large pot of water to a boil.

Lightly salt the boiling water, and add the pasta. Cook until al dente, according to package directions, about 6 to 8 minutes. While the pasta is still cooking, remove ¼ cup (60 ml) of the water from the pot, and set it aside.

Heat 1 tablespoon (15 ml) of extra-virgin olive oil and the onion in a large pan over medium-high heat. Fold in the spinach leaves, and sauté them for 2 minutes. Cover the pot with a lid and cook for 2 minutes, then season with the pinch of nutmeg, and sea salt and black pepper to taste.

Drain the pasta, and add it into the pan with the spinach mixture. Fold in the ricotta and Parmesan cheese, and pour in the reserved pasta cooking water. Cook all the ingredients for 2 minutes, or until the sauce is slightly reduced.

Remove the pan from the heat, add in the smoked salmon and lemon zest and toss gently to combine all the ingredients.

Serve immediately with black pepper on top.

Tip: *For an easy vegetarian version, substitute salmon with fresh mushrooms and Parmesan cheese with toasted breadcrumbs.*

Bucatini in Creamy Pea & Shrimp Sauce

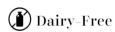 Dairy-Free

A delicious dinner doesn't need to take ages to prepare. This bucatini pasta in creamy pea and shrimp sauce is guaranteed to be on the table in less than fifteen minutes! Even better, there's absolutely no need to add cream or cheese to this pasta to reach that luscious, delicious texture, so it's also totally dairy-free.

I started making this pasta in an attempt to get my family to eat more vegetables, like these nutrient-packed peas, and it has always worked wonders. Then one night I had a bunch of friends coming over for a last-minute dinner, and after the initial panic of staring at an empty fridge, I grabbed a bag of frozen peas and some shrimp from the freezer, and this recipe was born.

Serves 4

12 oz (350 g) fresh or frozen peas

Zest of 1 lemon

1 tsp grated garlic

A pinch of red chili pepper flakes (optional)

2 tbsp (30 ml) extra-virgin olive oil, divided

Sea salt and freshly cracked black pepper

12 oz (350 g) bucatini pasta

7 oz (200 g) fresh shrimp, cleaned and deveined

Handful of toasted pistachios, crumbled (optional)

Bring a large pot of water to a boil.

Lightly salt the boiling water, add the peas and cook for about 2 to 3 minutes. Remove the peas with a slotted spoon and transfer them to a food processor or powerful blender. Reserve ¼ cup (60 ml) of the cooking water and set aside.

Add the lemon zest, garlic, chili flakes (if using) and 1 tablespoon (15 ml) of extra-virgin olive oil to the food processor together with the peas. Pulse to combine the ingredients. Pour in ¼ cup (60 ml) of the cooking water, and continue to blend until the pea cream reaches a smooth, dense consistency. Season to taste with sea salt and black pepper, and set aside until needed.

Add the pasta to the same water and same pot where the peas were boiled and cook until al dente, according to package directions, about 8 minutes. While the pasta is still cooking, remove ¼ cup (60 ml) of the water from the pot, and set it aside.

Heat the remaining extra-virgin olive oil in a large skillet over medium heat. Add the shrimp in a single layer, and stir-fry until cooked through, about 2 minutes. Remove half the shrimp from the pan, coarsely chop them with a sharp knife and return them to the skillet. Remove the skillet from the heat, and pour in the prepared pea cream.

Add the drained pasta to the skillet with the cooked shrimp and pea cream. Cook, tossing and adding the pasta cooking liquid as necessary, until the sauce is glossy and evenly coats the pasta, about 2 minutes.

Serve immediately with crumbled toasted pistachios (if using) and black pepper on top.

Classic Calamarata Pasta

🍶 **Dairy-Free**

As a proud Italian, I love cooking traditional recipes like this one; there's something magical in the way simple ingredients turn into mouthwatering delicacies, and this classic calamarata pasta is a perfect example.

Calamarata pasta inherited its name from calamari, because the round shape of the noodles resembles the rings of the popular squid dish. This super quick-and-easy summer pasta dish is traditionally cooked with tomatoes and, of course, fresh calamari.

Serves 4

2 whole fresh or defrosted calamari (about 2 cups [500 g], cleaned)

14 oz (400 g) calamarata bronze-died pasta

2 tbsp (30 ml) extra-virgin olive oil

1 clove garlic, finely minced

1 tbsp (15 g) double-concentrated tomato paste

¼ cup (60 ml) white wine

12 oz (350 g) cherry tomatoes, halved

Sea salt and freshly cracked black pepper

2 tbsp (5 g) fresh parsley leaves, finely chopped

Bring a large pot of water to a boil.

Rinse the calamari under cool running water, then pat them dry. Remove their heads (cut the eyes and mouth off), cut the tentacles off and set them aside. Remove the pen of the internal cartilage and the insides, then peel the skin off with your hands or a small knife.

Cut the calamari tubes into rings, similar in size to the calamarata pasta. Set them aside together with the reserved tentacles.

Lightly salt the boiling water, and add in the pasta. Cook until al dente, according to package directions, about 8 minutes. While the pasta is still cooking, remove ½ cup (120 ml) of the water from the pot, and set it aside.

Heat the extra-virgin olive oil in a large pan over medium-high heat. Fold in the calamari rings, tentacles and garlic and cook, stirring occasionally, for 2 minutes.

Mix the tomato paste with the wine, pour the mixture over the sides of the pan and allow the alcohol to evaporate. Fold in the tomatoes, season with sea salt and black pepper and cook over low heat for 5 minutes.

When the pasta finishes cooking, drain it and transfer it into the pan with the calamari sauce. Continue to cook, tossing and adding pasta cooking liquid as necessary, until the sauce is glossy and evenly coats the pasta, about 2 minutes.

Remove the pan from the heat. Top the pasta with the parsley and extra black pepper, and serve immediately.

Tip: *If you can't find the calamarata pasta, substitute with mezzi paccheri, paccheri or a similar short pasta shape.*

Classic Linguine alle Vongole

(*) Dairy-Free

Linguine alle vongole translates to "linguine with clams." It is a classic Italian summer dish. Every region has its own slightly adapted local version, and they're all insanely delicious—whether you go for the "red" (with tomatoes) or "white" (without) version. This white version is a favorite in my family. It's a simple yet elegant dish that makes lunch incredibly easy and totally amazing!

Serves 4

12 oz (350 g) linguine or spaghetti

4 tbsp (60 ml) extra-virgin olive oil

1 clove garlic

½ fresh red chili, deseeded and finely minced (optional)

2 lb (900 g) fresh clams, scrubbed and cleaned

4 tbsp (60 ml) fresh lemon juice

1 tbsp (4 g) fresh thyme leaves or chopped parsley, divided

Zest of 1 lemon (I recommend organic)

Freshly cracked black pepper

Bring a large pot of water to a boil.

Lightly salt the boiling water, and add the pasta. Cook until al dente, according to package directions, about 8 minutes. While the pasta is cooking, remove ¼ cup (60 ml) of the water from the pot, and set it aside.

Heat the extra-virgin olive oil in a large pan over medium-high heat. Add in the garlic and chili (if using), followed by the clams, and sauté all the ingredients for 2 minutes. Pour in the fresh lemon juice and ½ tablespoon (about 2 g) of the thyme leaves. Cover the pot with a lid and simmer until the clams open, about 2 minutes. Discard the garlic, chili and the clams that did not open. Pour the clam juice through a sieve, and set it aside.

Drain the pasta, and add it to the pan with the clams. Pour in the reserved filtered clam juice and pasta cooking water, and sauté all the ingredients for about 2 minutes.

Remove the pan from the heat, sprinkle with the lemon zest and the remaining thyme leaves and toss gently to combine all the ingredients.

Serve immediately with black pepper on top.

Tip: *I use white clams in this recipe, but littleneck or cockles will work well too.*

Speedy Spaghetti alla Nerano

Spaghetti alla Nerano may sound pompous, but it is a surprisingly simple and quick dish, featuring crispy thin zucchini slices and a magical cheesy sauce that will leave you hungry for more. The authentic spaghetti alla Nerano requires a specific cheese called Provolone del Monaco, but that cheese is as difficult to get as it is tasty, so I've swapped it with a more widely available combination of Pecorino Romano and Parmigiano Reggiano cheeses.

Serves 4

4 small zucchini

3 tbsp (45 ml) extra-virgin olive oil, plus more for frying

12 oz (350 g) spaghetti

1 clove garlic

6 tbsp (30 g) grated Pecorino Romano

⅔ cup (60 g) grated Parmesan cheese

Sea salt and freshly cracked black pepper

Handful of fresh basil leaves

Bring a large pot of water to a boil.

Finely slice the zucchini into rounds, and pat the slices dry with paper towels.

Heat plenty of olive oil in a large pan over medium heat. Add the zucchini in a single layer, and fry it until it's crispy and golden on both sides, about 2 minutes in total.

Remove the zucchini with a slotted spoon, and arrange the slices in a single layer on a dish covered with paper towels. Dab the slices with a paper towel to absorb the excess oil.

Lightly salt the boiling water, and add the pasta. Cook until al dente, according to package directions, about 8 minutes. While the pasta is cooking, remove ½ cup (120 ml) of the water from the pot, and set it aside.

Discard the frying oil from the pan. Add 3 tablespoons (45 ml) of fresh olive oil over medium-low heat. Add the garlic and cook until golden, about 2 minutes, then discard it. Drain the pasta, and add it into the pan with the garlic-infused olive oil.

Add the reserved cooking water, Pecorino, Parmesan and black pepper. Remove the pan from the heat, add the zucchini slices and basil leaves and toss gently to combine all the ingredients.

Serve immediately with extra black pepper on top.

Tips: *For best results, I recommend using spaghetti alla chitarra. It is similar to regular spaghetti but has a square shape that gives the pasta dish a lovely texture.*

Add a few fresh mint leaves for a vibrant twist.

Creamy Pumpkin & Smoked Pancetta Pasta

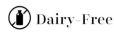 Dairy-Free

I'm so excited to show you how to make the most of any leftover Creamy Pumpkin Soup (page 27) by turning it into a gloriously comforting pasta dish that will warm you up on the coldest nights.

Don't skip using paccheri pasta if you can find it. The noodles have such a beautiful and practical shape that allows them to embrace the pumpkin cream and the crispy pancetta bits. Every bite of this pasta is guaranteed to be an explosion of flavor and texture!

Serves 4

12 oz (350 g) paccheri or other short pasta shape

1 tbsp (15 ml) extra-virgin olive oil

3½ oz (100 g) smoked pancetta, finely cubed

5 oz (150 g) leftover Creamy Pumpkin Soup (page 27)

½ tsp fresh thyme leaves

Sea salt and freshly cracked black pepper

Bring a large pot of water to a boil.

Lightly salt the boiling water, and add the pasta. Cook until al dente, according to package directions, about 8 minutes. While the pasta is cooking, remove ½ cup (120 ml) of the water from the pot, and set it aside.

Heat the extra-virgin olive oil in a large pan over medium heat, then add in the pancetta and stir-fry it until crispy, about 2 to 3 minutes. Remove the pancetta from the pan and set it aside. Pour the leftover pumpkin soup into the pan and heat over low heat.

Drain the pasta, and add it to the pan with the pumpkin soup. Pour in the reserved pasta cooking water and increase the heat to medium. Cook the pasta until the sauce is slightly thickened, then fold in the crispy pancetta and toss to combine all the ingredients.

Remove the pan from the heat. Sprinkle the thyme leaves over the pasta, and season with extra black pepper.

Tip: *For extra flavor, feel free to add some Parmesan cheese before serving this pasta.*

Pasta alla Boscaiola

🍶 Dairy-Free

This filling, heart-warming pasta is the kind of comfort food I crave when the temperature drops and it's just freezing out there.

This recipe is inspired by a traditional Italian pasta dish, *tagliatelle alla boscaiola,* which means "woodman's tagliatelle." This classic dish has many variations, but the most popular one includes wild or porcini mushrooms, Italian sausage and fresh double cream.

I wanted to lighten things up a little, so I've swapped the sausage with crispy Parma prosciutto and made a velvety, dairy-free sauce. And wow, I couldn't expect it to taste any better!

Serves 4

12 oz (350 g) bucatini pasta

2 tbsp (30 ml) extra-virgin olive oil

1 shallot, finely minced

10 oz (280 g) chanterelle mushrooms

Sea salt and freshly cracked black pepper

1 tbsp (6 g) all-purpose flour, sifted

⅓ cup (85 ml) warm vegetable stock

A pinch of nutmeg

4 thin slices Parma prosciutto

½ cup (30 g) fresh parsley leaves, finely minced

Bring a large pot of water to a boil.

Lightly salt the boiling water, and fold in the pasta. Cook until al dente, according to package directions, about 8 minutes. While the pasta is still cooking, remove ¼ cup (60 ml) of the water from the pot, and set it aside.

Heat 2 tablespoons (30 ml) of extra-virgin olive in a large pan over medium-low heat. Add the shallot and cook until it begins to turn golden, adding a bit of warm water if necessary.

Add the mushrooms to the pan and sauté them for 5 minutes over medium-high heat, or until cooked through. Season with sea salt and black pepper to taste.

Sprinkle the mushroom mixture with the flour, then pour in the warm stock and gently stir all the ingredients together. Continue to cook until the sauce thickens, about 2 minutes. Season with the nutmeg, and sea salt and black pepper to taste, and remove the pan from the heat.

Place the thin slices of Parma prosciutto in between paper towels, and microwave them on high heat for 1 minute. Remove the paper towel from the top, and allow the prosciutto slices to cool down and dry up for a couple of minutes, then break them into small bits.

Drain the pasta and add it to the pan with the chanterelle mushroom sauce. Pour in the reserved cooking water, and return to the heat. Cook until the sauce is velvety and creamy, about 2 minutes, tossing to combine all the ingredients.

Remove the pan from the heat, and stir in the crispy prosciutto bits and the parsley. Sprinkle with black pepper.

Quick Seafood Pasta

🍶 Dairy-Free

Pasta with seafood was a Sunday favorite growing up; my mum would make it with whatever fresh seafood she found at the big local Sunday fish market. This basic recipe can be easily customized with any kind of seafood you can get. To speed things up, I usually ask the fishmonger to clean the shrimp, calamari and mussels for me, so when I'm home I can get to the cooking straight away.

This fancy-looking seafood pasta is one of the easiest, most impressive meals you can put on the table in less than twenty minutes. It's insanely simple to put together and delivers bold, fresh seafood flavor. If you close your eyes, you can almost hear the sound of the sea!

Serves 4

12 oz (350 g) fresh homemade or dry spaghetti pasta

2 tbsp (30 ml) extra-virgin olive oil, divided

1 clove garlic

1 lb (450 g) fresh mussels, scrubbed and cleaned

½ cup (120 ml) white wine

14 oz (400 g) fresh calamari, cleaned and cut into rings

Handful of cherry tomatoes, halved and deseeded

8 fresh shrimp, cleaned

1 tsp double-concentrated tomato paste

1 tbsp (3 g) fresh parsley, finely chopped

Freshly cracked black pepper

Bring a large pot of water to a boil.

Lightly salt the boiling water, and add the pasta. Cook until al dente, according to package directions, about 6 to 8 minutes. While the pasta is still cooking, remove ¼ cup (60 ml) of the water from the pot, and set it aside.

Heat 1 tablespoon (15 ml) of the extra-virgin olive oil and the garlic clove in a large pot over medium-high heat. Add the mussels, followed by the white wine, and sauté them for 2 minutes. Cover the pot with a lid and simmer until the mussels open, about 2 minutes. Discard the garlic and mussels that did not open, then pour their juice through a sieve. Set aside both the cooked mussels and their filtered juice.

Return the pan to the heat with the remaining tablespoon (15 ml) of extra-virgin olive oil, add the calamari and tomatoes and sauté them for 2 minutes. Fold in the shrimp, and continue to cook all the ingredients for 4 to 5 minutes.

Drain the pasta, and add it into the pan with the calamari and shrimp. Fold in the mussels, then pour in the reserved filtered mussel juice, pasta cooking water and tomato paste. Sauté all the ingredients for about 2 minutes.

Remove the pan from the heat, sprinkle with the parsley and toss gently to combine all the ingredients.

Serve immediately with black pepper on top.

Easy Spaghetti alla Carrettiera

Need to feed a crowd in less than fifteen minutes? Spaghetti alla Carrettiera is the answer! The beauty of this dish comes from its simplicity. High-quality spaghetti, garlic, breadcrumbs, fresh tomatoes, anchovy fillets and aromatic fresh herbs come together in a big bowl of delicious awesomeness for the easiest pasta meal you could possibly make. It's perfect for novice cooks who want to impress their guests at their next dinner party!

Serves 4

12 oz (350 g) spaghetti

3 tbsp (45 ml) extra-virgin olive oil, divided

½ cup (60 g) panko breadcrumbs

2 tbsp (15 g) pine nuts

⅓ cup (30 g) sliced almonds

1 clove garlic, grated

2 anchovy fillets, rinsed and roughly chopped

½ tsp red chili pepper flakes

¾ cup (120 g) mini Piccadilly or cherry tomatoes, halved

Sea salt and freshly cracked black pepper

6 tbsp (30 g) grated Pecorino Romano cheese

1 tbsp (3 g) fresh parsley leaves, finely minced

1 tbsp (3 g) fresh basil leaves, finely minced

Bring a large pot of water to a boil. Lightly salt the boiling water, and add the pasta. Cook until al dente, according to package directions, about 8 minutes. While the pasta is cooking, remove ¼ cup (60 ml) of the water from the pot, and set it aside.

Heat 1 tablespoon (15 ml) of extra-virgin olive oil in a large pan over medium-low heat. Fold in the panko breadcrumbs, pine nuts and almonds, and toast until the nuts and breadcrumbs are golden brown. Remove all the ingredients from the pan, and set them aside.

Return the pan to medium heat, and pour in the remaining 2 tablespoons (30 ml) of extra-virgin olive oil. Add the garlic, anchovy fillets and chili flakes, and cook, stirring often, until the garlic just begins to turn golden, about 30 seconds. Fold in the tomatoes and allow to cook, stirring occasionally, for about 5 minutes. Season with sea salt and black pepper to taste, and remove from the heat.

Drain the pasta, add it to the pan with the tomato mixture and sprinkle with the Pecorino cheese. Pour in the reserved cooking water, then toss to combine all the ingredients.

Top the pasta with the breadcrumbs, pine nuts and almonds. Sprinkle with parsley and basil leaves, and serve immediately.

Tip: *I like to use pasta from Gragnano (a small town near Naples) whenever possible. The pasta there is made using a pasta machine and unique ingredients, which gives it a signature roughness and a porous surface that holds the sauce so much better!*

Asparagus & Pea Risotto

🌾 Gluten-Free

One of the best things about being a food blogger is that you get to go to lots of exciting foodie events. Over the years, I've had the opportunity to chat with and cook alongside some of the most famous chefs in Italy and the U.K., and I've learned a trick or two about how to make a quick, awesome risotto at home. Turns out that stirring the risotto during the cooking process with a whisk and not with a wooden spoon helps incredibly in the final effect of the dish, as it allows the starch to be released and thoroughly bind everything together. This luxurious yet extremely easy asparagus and pea risotto is delicate but incredibly aromatic. It's one of those perfect meals to celebrate the spring season.

Serves 4

4 cups (1 L) vegetable stock

8 fresh asparagus

7 oz (200 g) fresh or defrosted peas

2 tbsp (30 ml) extra-virgin olive oil

1 shallot, finely minced

1 tbsp + ½ tbsp (15 g + 7 g) good-quality butter, divided

1 tsp fresh thyme leaves

Sea salt and freshly cracked black pepper

10½ oz (300 g) vialone nano or carnaroli rice

¼ cup (60 ml) good-quality white wine

Juice of ½ lemon

Zest of 1 lemon, divided

3 tbsp (15 g) grated Parmesan cheese

Place the stock in a small pot, and bring to a gentle boil. Finely cube the asparagus stems and cut the spears in half lengthwise. Then add them together with the peas into the boiling stock, and cook for 4 minutes. Turn the heat off, and cover the pot with a lid to keep the stock warm.

Heat a small pan with the extra-virgin olive oil over medium-high heat. Add the shallot and sauté gently until soft, about 2 minutes. Remove the asparagus and peas from the pot with a slotted spoon, and transfer them to the pan with the sweated shallot. Add in ½ tablespoon (7 g) of butter and the thyme leaves, and sauté the vegetables for 2 minutes. Season with sea salt and black pepper to taste, and remove from the heat.

Heat a large pan over low heat. Add the rice and toast it for 2 to 3 minutes, or until it has turned translucent, stirring continuously with a wooden spoon to avoid burning it. Add the wine, turn up the heat to medium-high and allow it to evaporate. Return the heat to medium-low, add the lemon juice, half of the lemon zest and one ladle of stock, and allow the rice to absorb it. Continue to cook, gradually adding the stock, whisking constantly with a whisk until the rice is soft but still has a bite, about 15 minutes. Fold the cooked asparagus and peas into the pan in the last 2 minutes of cooking time, and stir to combine all the ingredients.

Remove the risotto from the heat, stir in the Parmesan cheese, the remaining butter and lemon zest, then shake the pan vigorously to combine all the ingredients. The risotto should reach a smooth and creamy consistency. Divide the risotto among plates, and serve immediately.

Tip: *I like to use a silicone whisk when making risotto, but you can totally use a regular metal whisk. Just make sure to whisk your risotto delicately to avoid scraping the pan.*

Porcini, Leek & Prosciutto Risotto

(🌾) Gluten-Free

This risotto is the kind of heart-warming comfort food I could eat all winter long. It's creamy, umami-rich thanks to the luxurious porcini mushrooms, and the crunchy topping of savory Parma prosciutto brings everything to the next level, making a wonderful restaurant-worthy meal in barely twenty minutes.

Serves 4

4 cups (1 L) vegetable stock

2 tbsp (30 ml) extra-virgin olive oil

1 shallot, finely minced

1 leek, finely chopped

5 oz (150 g) fresh porcini mushrooms, roughly chopped

Sea salt and freshly cracked black pepper

10½ oz (300 g) vialone nano or carnaroli rice

¼ cup (60 ml) good-quality white wine

4 thin slices Parma prosciutto

3 tbsp (15 g) grated Parmesan cheese

1 tbsp (15 g) good-quality butter

Place the stock in a small pot, and keep it warm over a gentle heat.

Heat a small pan with the extra-virgin olive oil over medium-high heat. Add in the shallot, leek and mushrooms, and sauté gently for about 5 minutes, stirring occasionally. Season with sea salt and black pepper.

In the meantime, heat a large pan over low heat. Add the rice and toast it for 2 to 3 minutes, stirring continuously with a wooden spoon to avoid burning it, or until it has turned translucent. Add the wine, turn up the heat to medium-high and allow it to evaporate. Return the heat to medium-low, then pour in one ladle of stock, and allow the rice to absorb it. Season with sea salt to taste.

Stir the sautéed mushrooms into the pan with the risotto, and continue to cook, gradually adding in stock and whisking constantly with a whisk until the rice is soft but still has a bite, about 15 minutes.

In the meantime, place the thin slices of Parma prosciutto in between two pieces of paper towels and microwave them on high heat for 1 minute. Remove the paper towel from the top, and allow the prosciutto slices to cool down and dry up for a couple of minutes, then break them into small bits.

Remove the risotto from the heat. Add in the Parmesan cheese, butter and crispy prosciutto, then shake the pan vigorously to combine all the ingredients. The risotto should reach a smooth and creamy consistency.

Divide the risotto among plates, and serve it immediately.

Tip: *It's not easy to find fresh Italian porcini mushrooms, so feel free to substitute with a mix of wild mushrooms such as shiitake or chanterelles.*

Lemon Risotto with Shrimp Tartare

(🌾) Gluten-Free

This is a simple, delicate yet impressive dish that I often prepare when I have guests coming over for dinner. Make sure to use super fresh shrimp for the tartare—no compromises here. To cut prep time, ask your fishmonger to clean them up for you. I also recommend you use a good-quality rice when making risotto. Both vialone nano or carnaroli would work well, and if you want to go a step further, opt for the famous Acquerello rice (an aged carnaroli variety super popular among Michelin-starred chefs). Remember, one of the keys for a great risotto with perfect creamy texture is to stir continuously throughout the cooking time and also to vigorously shake the pan when it's done.

Serves 4

4 cups (1 L) vegetable or fish stock

2 tbsp (30 ml) extra-virgin olive oil, divided

1 shallot, finely minced

10½ oz (300 g) vialone nano or carnaroli rice

¼ cup (60 ml) good-quality white wine

Zest and juice of 1 lemon, divided

Sea salt

8–10 large fresh shrimp, cleaned and finely chopped

1 tsp fresh thyme leaves

Freshly cracked black pepper

3 tbsp (15 g) grated Parmesan cheese

1 tbsp (15 g) good-quality butter

Place the stock in a small pot, and keep it warm over a gentle heat.

Heat a small pan with 1 tablespoon (15 ml) of extra-virgin olive oil over medium-high heat. Add the shallot and gently sauté until soft, about 2 minutes.

Heat a large pan over low heat. Add the rice and toast it for 2 to 3 minutes, or until it has turned translucent, stirring continuously with a wooden spoon to avoid burning it. Add the wine, turn up the heat to medium-high and allow it to evaporate.

Return the heat to medium-low, then add half the lemon juice, one-third of the zest and one ladle of stock, and allow the rice to absorb it. Season with sea salt to taste. Stir in the cooked shallot, and continue to cook, gradually adding stock and whisking constantly with a whisk until the rice is soft but still has a bite, about 15 minutes.

In a small bowl combine the shrimp with the remaining tablespoon (15 ml) of extra-virgin olive oil, the remaining lemon juice, one-third of the zest and thyme leaves. Season with sea salt and black pepper to taste, and refrigerate until ready to serve.

Remove the risotto from the heat, add in the Parmesan cheese, butter and remaining lemon zest, then shake the pan vigorously to combine all the ingredients. The risotto should reach a smooth and creamy consistency.

Divide the risotto among plates, top each plate with a quarter of the shrimp tartare and serve it immediately.

Tip: *Although it might be a bit hard to find, swap in lemon thyme if you can find it.*

Shiitake Mushroom, Pumpkin & Rosemary Risotto

🌾 Gluten-Free

In Northern Italy, risotto is considered a simple, everyday comfort food. For me, it's something to prepare mostly on special occasions, or for a cozy dinner date with my better half. Among all the risotto recipes I've made over the years, this is probably my favorite. When pumpkin and mushroom season finally hits, I make this risotto on repeat! Any kind of mushrooms will work here; I like to use fresh shiitake mushrooms because they can be found easily at the market and vaguely remind me of delicious, hard-to-find, expensive Italian porcini mushrooms. A mix of wild and porcini mushrooms would work well too.

Serves 4

4 cups (1 L) vegetable stock

2 tbsp (30 ml) extra-virgin olive oil

1 shallot, finely minced

5 oz (150 g) shiitake or wild mushrooms, roughly chopped

5 oz (150 g) muscat or Hokkaido pumpkin flesh, finely cubed

Sea salt and freshly cracked black pepper

10½ oz (300 g) vialone nano or carnaroli rice

¼ cup (60 ml) good-quality white wine

3 tbsp (15 g) grated Parmesan cheese

1 tbsp (15 g) good-quality butter

1 tsp fresh rosemary leaves, finely minced

Place the stock in a small pot, and keep it warm over a gentle heat.

Heat a small pan with the extra-virgin olive oil over medium-high heat. Add the shallot, mushrooms and pumpkin and sauté gently for about 5 minutes, stirring occasionally. Season with sea salt and black pepper.

In the meantime, heat a large pan over low heat. Add the rice and toast it for 2 to 3 minutes, or until it has turned translucent, stirring continuously with a wooden spoon to avoid burning it. Add the wine, turn up the heat to medium-high and allow it to evaporate. Return the heat to medium-low, then pour in one ladle of stock, and allow the rice to absorb it. Season with salt to taste.

Stir the sautéed vegetables into the pan with the risotto, and continue to cook, gradually adding in stock and whisking constantly with a whisk until the rice is soft but still has a bite, about 15 minutes.

Remove the risotto from the heat, add in the Parmesan cheese, butter and rosemary, then shake the pan vigorously to combine all the ingredients. The risotto should reach a smooth consistency.

Divide the risotto among plates, and serve it immediately.

Tip: *I like this risotto less creamy than the classic risotto, but if you want it super gooey and rich, add an extra pat or two of butter. If you have a hard time finding muscat pumpkin, substitute with Hokkaido pumpkin.*

Perfect Meat & Poultry Dishes in No Time

If you've ever thought that Italian meat and poultry mains take ages to prepare, think again. Quick-and-easy Italian *secondi*—that's what we call our main courses—are totally possible.

My parents are both masters of fast, inexpensive meals. I grew up with the speedy nutritious meals you'll find in this chapter, including my dad's veal scaloppine (featured on page 82, made with a white wine sauce for a grown-up version) and my mum's Quick Lemon Chicken Piccata (page 77). I now make these delicious dishes on a weekly basis for my family too, and I'm forever grateful to my parents for teaching me these lifesaving recipes!

Quick Lemon Chicken Piccata

Lemon chicken piccata is an impressive yet simple classic recipe that gets dinner on the table in just fifteen minutes!

Piccata is an Italian cooking technique where the meat is sliced, gently coated in flour, stir-fried and served with a sauce made from the pan drippings with added lemon, capers, wine, shallots and butter. Although in Italy the most famous version is veal piccata, the chicken variation is even better!

Serves 4

4 medium-small skinless chicken breasts

Sea salt and freshly cracked black pepper

½ cup (60 g) all-purpose flour

2 tbsp (30 ml) extra-virgin olive oil

3 tbsp (45 g) butter, divided

3 tbsp (45 ml) fresh lemon juice

¼ cup (60 ml) chicken stock

2 tbsp (15 g) salt-preserved capers, rinsed

1 shallot, finely minced

2 fresh thyme sprigs, leaves only

1 tbsp (3 g) fresh parsley or more thyme leaves, finely chopped

Place 1 chicken breast inside a large zip-top bag and seal the bag, pressing out as much air as possible. Pound the chicken using a rolling pin to an even ½-inch (1-cm) thickness. Repeat the process with the remaining chicken breasts.

Season the chicken breasts generously with sea salt and black pepper. Place the flour in a bowl. Dredge each chicken breast in the flour, shake off the excess and set the meat aside.

Heat the extra-virgin olive oil and half of the butter in a medium frying pan over medium-high heat. Add the chicken breasts and cook for 2 to 3 minutes on each side. Transfer them to a plate, and cover with foil.

Pour the lemon juice and chicken stock into the hot pan and gently scrape the bottom of the pan with a wooden spoon. Fold in the capers, shallot and thyme leaves, and bring the mixture to a gentle boil. Return the chicken breasts to the pan, and simmer all the ingredients for 5 minutes.

Remove the chicken breasts from the pan, and arrange them on a serving plate.

Add the remaining butter to the sauce and whisk all the ingredients for about a minute, until it reaches a silky, smooth consistency.

Pour the sauce over the chicken breasts. Garnish with parsley or extra thyme leaves and black pepper.

Tip: *For extra flavor, replace the chicken stock with some leftover good-quality white wine.*

Chicken Prosciutto Saltimbocca

The Italian word *saltimbocca* literally means "a jump in the mouth," which is apt because your taste buds will jump for joy when you taste the incredible flavors in this dish. The traditional recipe calls for thinly sliced veal, but I find that this super quick-and-easy version is a fantastic way to bring plain chicken breast from boring to amazing.

Serves 4

2½ tbsp (20 g) all-purpose flour (I recommend organic)

4 (3½-oz [100-g]) thin chicken breast cutlets

4 slices Parma prosciutto

4 large fresh sage leaves

3 tbsp (45 ml) extra-virgin olive oil

Freshly cracked black pepper

1 tbsp (15 g) butter

A splash of white wine

Arrange the flour in a shallow dish. Dip each chicken cutlet into the flour and coat evenly, then shake off the excess and arrange the cutlets on a chopping board. Gently layer a slice of Parma prosciutto onto each cutlet, top with a sage leaf and secure with a cocktail stick.

Heat the extra-virgin olive oil in a large nonstick frying pan over medium heat. Add the chicken cutlets in a single layer, ham side down. Sear the chicken cutlets for 2 minutes, until the bottom is colored and crispy. Flip the chicken cutlets, and season with pepper. Continue searing for 3 more minutes, until the bottom is browned and the chicken is cooked through. Remove from the pan, arrange the chicken saltimbocca on a plate and cover with foil to keep warm.

Add the butter to the pan and cook until foamy. Pour in the wine and shake the pan vigorously until the sauce reaches a velvety consistency. Divide the chicken saltimbocca between four plates, pour the sauce on top and serve immediately.

Tip: *For the traditional version, substitute chicken with veal. For stronger flavors, substitute sage with rosemary sprigs.*

Easiest–Ever Beer Chicken Skewers

🍾 Dairy–Free

Juicy, tender, aromatic and packed with a lovely citrusy aroma and a deep amber beer flavor, these chicken skewers have all it takes to leave you hungry for more!

The marinade comes together in a blink, so you can soak the skewers for as long as possible before grilling them. I tend not to skip the marinating process when grilling meat, even when all I've got is just twenty minutes to get dinner on the table.

I like to use an Italian amber beer for the marinade, which adds hints of caramel. For a more subtle beer flavor, feel free to substitute it with a blonde beer.

I often make these skewers on their own, but they are just as great with some extra veggies, such as zucchini, onion and peppers skewered between the chicken pieces.

Serves 4

2 tbsp (30 ml) extra-virgin olive oil

Juice of ½ lemon

Juice of ½ orange

2 cloves garlic, halved

1 red chili pepper, deseeded and halved lengthwise

Sea salt and freshly cracked white pepper

1 lb (450 g) chicken breast, cut into 1-inch (2½-cm) cubes

½ cup (120 ml) artisanal amber (or blonde) beer

1 tbsp (3 g) fresh parsley, finely chopped

1 lemon or lime, cut into wedges

In a large baking dish, mix together the extra-virgin olive oil with the juice of the lemon and orange, the garlic and the chili. Season generously with sea salt and white pepper to taste, and set the marinade aside until needed.

Thread the chicken cubes loosely onto metal or bamboo skewers, and place them in the baking dish with the marinade. Pour the beer all over, and stir to combine all the ingredients. Cover the baking dish with plastic wrap, and refrigerate for at least 10 minutes.

Heat a large grilling pan over medium heat until hot. Add the chicken skewers and let them cook for 2 minutes on each side, brushing the leftover marinade over them as they cook, until the meat is cooked through, about 5 minutes.

Remove the skewers from the pan and arrange them on a serving plate. Sprinkle the parsley on top, and serve with lemon wedges on the side.

Tips: *To make this recipe lighter, I've used chicken breast. I also recommend boneless, skinless chicken thighs, which are more flavorful than chicken breasts and easier to cook without drying the meat out.*

If you're using bamboo skewers, soak your sticks in water for at least 5 minutes to prevent burning before threading the chicken cubes onto them.

White Wine Veal Scaloppine

Veal scaloppine is one of the easiest, quickest and tastiest Italian recipes you can pull together for a last-minute dinner. A few moments in the pan, a couple ingredients to create a velvety flavorful sauce and voilà, dinner is ready in a blink. All you need is some crusty bread or some Speedy Pan-Roasted New Potatoes (page 157) on the side, and you've got yourself a tasty Italian-style dinner in no time.

Serves 4

1 lb (450 g) veal cutlets, also called scaloppine

Sea salt and freshly cracked black pepper

½ cup (60 g) all-purpose flour

2 tbsp (30 ml) extra-virgin olive oil

2 tbsp (30 g) butter, divided

½ cup (120 ml) white wine

Juice of ½ lemon

¼ cup (60 ml) chicken stock

1 tbsp (3 g) fresh parsley, finely chopped

Place 1 veal cutlet inside a large zip-top bag and seal the bag, pressing out as much air as possible. Pound the beef using a rolling pin to an even ½-inch (1-cm) thickness. Repeat the process with the remaining slices.

Season the veal generously with sea salt and black pepper. Place the flour in a bowl and dredge each cutlet in the flour, shake off the excess and set the meat aside.

Heat the extra-virgin olive oil and half of the butter in a medium frying pan over medium-high heat. Add the veal cutlets and cook for 2 minutes, turning them once, until browned on both sides. Transfer them to a serving plate, and cover with foil.

Pour the white wine into the pan and allow it to evaporate over high heat. Pour in the lemon juice and stock, gently scraping the bottom of the pan with a wooden spoon, and bring the mixture to a boil.

Add the remaining butter to the sauce and whisk all the ingredients for about a minute, until it reaches a silky, smooth consistency.

Pour the sauce over the veal scaloppine and sprinkle with parsley and black pepper.

Fast & Luscious Marinated Beef Skewers

  Dairy-Free, Gluten-Free

No summer barbecue is complete without these juicy, tender and quickly marinated beef skewers! I always like to add a bit of marinating time to any meat I'm about to grill, and even though it's usually best to leave the meat to marinate for a few hours, my motto is a little marinating time is better than no marinating at all!

These skewers are super simple, flavorful and packed with veggies. Feel totally free to use only one or two veggies listed below, or substitute with your favorite ones. You can also add a mix of different meat: sausage, veal and chicken would work great!

Serves 4 to 6

3 tbsp (45 ml) extra-virgin olive oil

1 clove garlic, grated

1 tbsp (3 g) rosemary leaves, finely chopped

4 sage leaves, finely chopped

1 tsp thyme leaves

Sea salt and freshly cracked black pepper

1 lb (450 g) beef fillet, cut into 1-inch (2½-cm) cubes

1 red bell pepper, cut into 1-inch (2½-cm) squares

1 yellow bell pepper, cut into 1-inch (2½-cm) squares

1 small zucchini, cut into 1-inch (2½-cm) rounds

1 lemon, cut into wedges, for serving

In a small bowl, mix together the extra-virgin olive oil with the garlic and herbs. Season generously with sea salt and black pepper to taste, and set the marinade aside until needed.

Loosely thread the beef and vegetables, alternating them, onto metal or bamboo skewers, and arrange them in a casserole dish.

Drizzle the marinade all over the skewers, cover the dish with plastic wrap and place it in the refrigerator for at least 10 minutes.

Heat a large grilling pan over medium heat until hot. Add the beef skewers and let them cook for 2 minutes on each side, brushing the leftover marinade over them as they cook, until the meat reaches your desired level of doneness.

Remove the skewers from the pan, arrange them on a serving plate and serve with lemon wedges on the side.

Tip: *You may also grill these beef skewers in the oven. Preheat the oven to 400°F (200°C, or gas mark 6) and grill them for about 15 minutes or until fully cooked, turning the skewers halfway through cooking them.*

If you're using bamboo skewers, soak your sticks in water for at least 5 minutes to prevent burning before threading the meat and vegetables onto them.

Classic Italian Polpette (Meatballs)

This book wouldn't be properly Italian if I didn't include a foolproof recipe for classic Italian meatballs! So, here you go—these are my all-time favorite beef meatballs. The recipe is inspired by my mum's delicious meatballs and a few tricks my dear friend and *MasterChef*—winner Luca Manfè taught me a few years ago when he gave me his own mum's precious meatball recipe. This unique version of Italian polpette features some of my favorite flavors, such as lemon zest, garlic and white wine, which you can totally omit if you prefer a more delicate flavor.

Serves 4

2 thick slices rustic ciabatta bread

½ cup (120 ml) milk

1 large egg, beaten

1 cup (100 g) panko breadcrumbs

4 tbsp (22 g) grated Parmesan cheese

1 tsp minced garlic

2 tsp (10 ml) good-quality white wine

1 tbsp (3 g) fresh parsley, finely minced

1 tsp lemon zest

1 tsp fresh thyme leaves

10½ oz (300 g) ground beef

Sea salt and freshly cracked black pepper

3 tbsp (23 g) all-purpose flour

4 tbsp (60 ml) extra-virgin olive oil

Cut the bread into small cubes, and place them in a bowl with the milk. Allow the bread to sit for a few minutes, then drain it and squeeze out the excess milk with your hands, and place the bread in a large bowl. Add in the egg, panko breadcrumbs, Parmesan cheese, garlic, white wine, parsley, lemon zest and thyme. Combine all the ingredients. Add the ground beef, and season generously with sea salt and black pepper. Mix gently, but thoroughly, with your hands to combine all the ingredients.

Take a small piece of the meat mixture and gently roll it between your hands to form 1-inch (2½-cm) meatballs (about 1 full tablespoon [15 g] each).

Place the flour in a shallow dish. Roll the meatball gently into the flour until lightly covered, arrange it on a baking tray and flatten it lightly with the palm of your hand. Repeat the process until all the meat mixture is used.

Heat the extra-virgin olive oil in a large frying pan over medium heat. Fold in the meatballs and leave them undisturbed until they are brown on one side. Shake the pan to loosen the meatballs, then turn each one with tongs to cook on the other side for 3 to 4 minutes.

Remove the meatballs from the heat, and arrange them on a plate covered with paper towels to absorb the excess oil. Transfer the meatballs to a large serving plate.

Tip: *Use leftover meatballs to make an awesome pasta with meatball and tomato sauce the next day!*

Easy Awesome Beer Turkey Meatballs

I love prepping all sorts of meatballs: they're easy, comforting and take no time to prepare. But I tend to make these beer turkey meatballs more than any other meatball recipe because my family goes absolutely crazy over them—dueling with forks over the last meatball kind of crazy. The beer adds such a delicate, refreshing aroma to the luscious, velvety sauce, and the meatballs explode with flavor in your mouth.

For soft, full-of-texture meatballs, I like to add some leftover steamed floury potato (Russet potatoes work great!) into the meatball mix. If you don't have it on hand, you can substitute with a thick slice of ciabatta bread briefly dipped into milk and torn by hand. And if you want to add an extra layer of flavor, sneak a tiny bit of good-quality organic butter into the sauce right before serving.

Serves 4

1 large egg, beaten

1 cup (100 g) panko breadcrumbs

4 tbsp (22 g) grated Parmesan cheese

1 medium-small steamed floury potato (such as Russet), peeled and chopped

1 tbsp (3 g) fresh parsley leaves, finely minced (plus more for serving, optional)

10½ oz (300 g) ground turkey meat

Sea salt and freshly cracked black pepper

3 tbsp (23 g) all-purpose flour

3 tbsp (45 ml) extra-virgin olive oil

1 shallot, finely sliced

5 fl oz (150 ml) good-quality blonde beer

In a large bowl, combine the egg, panko breadcrumbs, Parmesan cheese, potato and parsley. Add the ground turkey, and season generously with sea salt and black pepper. Mix gently, but thoroughly, with your hands to combine all the ingredients.

Take a small piece of the meat mixture, and gently roll it between your hands to form 1-inch (2½-cm) meatballs (about 1 full tablespoon [15 g] each).

Place the flour into a shallow dish. Roll the meatball gently in the flour until lightly covered, and arrange it on a baking tray. Repeat the process until all the meat mixture is used.

Heat the extra-virgin olive oil in a large frying pan over medium heat. Add the shallot, and cook until softened, about 2 minutes. Add the meatballs and leave them undisturbed until they are brown on one side. Shake the pan to loosen the meatballs, then turn each one with tongs to brown the other side. Keep turning with tongs until they are completely and evenly browned.

Pour the beer into the pan and cook over high heat for 2 minutes. Cover the pan with a lid and continue to cook for 5 minutes, or until the sauce is reduced to your desired consistency.

Top with extra parsley and black pepper if desired.

Tip: *You can also freeze these meatballs for a quick last-minute dinner. Thaw in the fridge overnight before using them.*

Fast Oven-Baked Chicken Cotolette (Breaded Chicken Cutlets)

Chicken cotoletta is basically the Italian version of breaded chicken. This is the kind of comfort food I grew up with; every Italian family has a personal version of cotoletta, and they all taste equally good. This version I'm sharing is inspired by my mum's chicken cotoletta: She adds garlic, aromatic herbs and a generous grating of Parmigiano Reggiano into the coating mix, then fries the cotolette until golden and crispy. I pretty much follow her recipe, but I prefer a quick oven-baked version for a lighter meal. To make my life easier, I also use panko breadcrumbs instead of Italian breadcrumbs from the bakery. I've been living in the U.K. for a long time and it's not easy to find the same quality of breadcrumb. I find that using panko breadcrumbs is a good compromise and consistently delivers, whether you live in London, Los Angeles or Milan.

These chicken cotolette make a lovely meal all year round. I like to serve them along with a vibrant New Potato, Green Bean & Tuna Salad (page 147) in winter time or paired with a ten-minute panzanella (page 11) for a nutritious summer meal.

Serves 4

4 tbsp (60 ml) extra-virgin olive oil, divided

4 (1-inch [2½-cm]) slices chicken breast (I recommend organic)

Sea salt and freshly cracked black pepper

2 medium eggs (I recommend organic)

¾ cup (85 g) panko breadcrumbs

4 tbsp (22 g) grated Parmesan cheese

½ clove garlic, grated

2 tbsp (5 g) fresh parsley, finely chopped

1 lemon, cut into wedges

Preheat the oven to 375°F (190°C, or gas mark 5). Line a large baking tray with baking paper, and brush with half the extra-virgin olive oil.

Season the chicken slices with sea salt and black pepper on both sides. Whisk the eggs on a large, shallow plate.

Combine the panko breadcrumbs, Parmesan cheese, garlic and parsley in a separate plate. Season with sea salt and black pepper to taste.

Dip each chicken slice in the egg mixture, then dredge it in the seasoned bread-crumbs until fully coated. Place the chicken cotolette onto the prepared baking tray, and drizzle the remaining extra-virgin olive oil on top of them.

Bake for about 15 minutes, turning them halfway through cooking, or until crispy and golden on top. Remove the chicken cotolette from the oven, arrange them on a serving plate and serve with lemon wedges on the side.

Tip: *Panko breadcrumbs are available in most major supermarkets and Asian food stores. For extra flavor, try substituting the Parmesan cheese with Pecorino Romano.*

Exciting Fish & Seafood Mains in a Blink

Growing up in Sicily, a step away from the sea, it was an obvious choice for my family to eat as much fresh fish and seafood as possible. My mum would go to the fish market almost every day to get the catch of the day and make us delicious, healthy and speedy meals such as Grilled Squid with Salmoriglio Dressing (page 107) or Fish in Crazy Water (page 104).

My love for fish and seafood dishes has only grown over the years, so it was pretty hard to put together a handpicked selection of the recipes that I love the most. But I'm confident I've chosen the right ones to whet your appetite and to make sure you have a delightful meal to enjoy with your family in just a few minutes.

From flavorful Sicilian classic recipes such as the Aeolian-Style Pan-Roasted Cod Fillet (page 96), to creative and totally restaurant-worthy dishes such as Pistachio-Crusted Tuna with Orange Sauce (page 95), there's a wealth of tasty, quick ideas for both everyday meals and special occasions.

Pistachio-Crusted Tuna with Orange Sauce

 Dairy-Free

This is the kind of meal I often order at Sicilian restaurants, and I usually prepare it on special occasions for my other half. It's perfect because, even after a long tiring day at work, it can be put together in fifteen minutes and look like you spent hours on it! The ingredient combination tastes as good as it looks and screams Sicily all over: seared fresh tuna with a crunchy, sweet coating of pistachios, served with a luscious, velvety orange salsa for a refreshing touch. I promise, this simple-yet-elegant meal is sure to wow your dinner date!

Serves 4

3½ tbsp (52 ml) extra-virgin olive oil, divided

½ tbsp (4 g) all-purpose flour (I recommend organic)

Juice of 2 oranges (I recommend organic)

1 tbsp (15 ml) water

Sea salt

4 (6-oz [180-g]) sashimi-grade tuna fillets, cut about 2 inches (5 cm) thick

2 cups (240 g) unsalted pistachios, finely crumbled

2 tbsp (8 g) pistachio flour

Zest of ½ lemon

Heat a small pan over low heat and add 1½ tablespoons (22 ml) of the extra-virgin olive oil and the flour. Whisk until combined. Remove the pan from the heat and pour in the orange juice and 1 tablespoon (15 ml) of water. Season with sea salt to taste, and return the pan to the heat. Cook the sauce, stirring constantly, until it thickens to your desired consistency, about 1 to 2 minutes. Remove the sauce from the heat, and set it aside until ready to serve.

Brush the tuna with the remaining 2 tablespoons (30 ml) of extra-virgin olive oil. Heat a large grilling pan over medium-low heat. Add the tuna and cook for 2 minutes on each side, or until it reaches the desired degree of doneness.

In a large, shallow dish, combine the crumbled pistachios, pistachio flour, lemon zest and a generous pinch of sea salt.

Remove the fish from the pan, then dredge all sides of each fillet in the pistachio mixture. Repeat the process with the remaining tuna, then cut into thick slices and serve with the sauce on the side.

Tips: *The tuna fillets are gently seared, so make sure to buy sashimi-grade sustainably sourced tuna for the best results.*

If you can find them easily, use Sicilian Bronte pistachios. They have a unique sweetness, moist texture and an incredibly rich flavor!

Aeolian-Style Pan-Roasted Cod Fillet

🍾 🌾 Dairy-Free, Gluten-Free

This dish brings me back to my childhood Sicilian summers, when my family and I used to spend our holidays each year at a different Aeolian island, usually Vulcano, Filicudi or Salina. While there, we lived in a sort of island bubble, savoring each and every day spent at the beach and all the precious moments spent cooking and eating the local specialties together. Aeolian-style dishes usually feature a simple, quick sauce made with local olives, capers, cherry tomatoes and bits of wild fennel tips, if available—which I've omitted here because they're darn hard to find outside of Sicily!

I've used cod fillets for this simple version, because they're inexpensive and widely available. If you can get your hands on a fresh swordfish steak, then go for it—it will taste amazing!

Serves 4

4 tbsp (60 ml) extra-virgin olive oil, divided

1 small red onion, finely minced

2½ tbsp (15 g) fresh celery, finely chopped

10½ oz (300 g) ripe small Piccadilly or cherry tomatoes, halved

1 tsp salt-preserved capers, rinsed

1 tsp freshly dried oregano leaves

8 Sicilian black olives or Greek Kalamata olives

Sea salt and freshly cracked black pepper

4 (4½-oz [125-g]) fresh cod fillets

Handful of fresh baby basil leaves or fennel tops

Heat 3 tablespoons (45 ml) of extra-virgin olive oil in a large sauté pan over medium heat. Add the onion and celery. Cook, stirring often, for about 2 minutes, adding a little water if necessary.

Fold in the tomatoes, capers, oregano and olives. Cover with a lid and allow to cook, stirring occasionally, for about 10 minutes.

Taste the sauce and season accordingly with sea salt and black pepper. Then, with the help of a spatula, push the tomatoes to the edges of the pan.

Brush the skin of the fish with the remaining extra-virgin olive oil, and place the fillets skin side down in the pan. Season them with a pinch of salt, then cover with a lid and cook for about 4 minutes, or until the fish is cooked through and fully opaque.

Once the fish is ready, remove the fillets with a spatula and divide among four plates. Pour a ladle of the Aeolian sauce on each fish fillet, top with chopped basil and serve immediately.

Black Pepper Mussels

  Dairy-Free, Gluten-Free

In Italy, any restaurant on the seaside has Black Pepper Mussels on the menu. Sometimes they're served in a red version with chopped tomatoes, but you can't go wrong by re-creating the simple white version featured here. There's everything to love about this dish—it's quick to make, inexpensive and loaded with sea flavors. An absolute must-try dish for the summer season!

Serves 4

4 lb (1.8 kg) fresh mussels, cleaned

Freshly cracked black pepper

Handful of fresh parsley, finely chopped

2 lemons, cut into wedges

Heat a large pot over medium-high heat. Add the mussels and season with a generous amount of black pepper. Cover the pan with a lid and cook for 3 to 4 minutes, shaking the pan occasionally.

Remove the pot from the heat, and discard the mussels that did not open.

Transfer the mussels and any juices onto a serving plate, sprinkle the parsley all over them and serve with lemon wedges on the side.

Crispy Lemon Cod Fish Balls

🍼 Dairy-Free

These light and crispy lemon cod fish balls only require a handful of ingredients, and they make the most of any leftover cooked potatoes and fish you have in the fridge. Did I mention they are conveniently baked instead of fried? How awesome is that? Serve them with a refreshing, homemade garlicky yogurt dip or with some organic ketchup for a perfect appetizer to share.

Serves 4

1 medium floury potato (such as Russet), peeled and steamed

10½ oz (300 g) fresh or frozen cod fillets, steamed

1 tbsp (3 g) fresh parsley, finely chopped

Zest of 1 lemon (I recommend organic)

Sea salt and freshly cracked black pepper

¼ cup (30 g) panko breadcrumbs

1 tbsp (15 ml) extra-virgin olive oil, plus extra for greasing

2 free-range egg whites

For the Garlic Yogurt Dip

3½ oz (100 g) plain or dairy-free yogurt

Zest of ½ lemon (I recommend organic)

1 clove garlic, finely grated

Sea salt and freshly cracked black pepper

Preheat the oven to 350°F (175°C, or gas mark 4), and arrange a baking tray on the top shelf.

In a large bowl, mash the potato with a fork, then fold in the steamed cod fillets, parsley and lemon zest. Season with sea salt and black pepper to taste, and mix all the ingredients with your hands until combined. Shape your prepared fish ball–mixture into small, even balls. You should be able to make around 15 golf ball–sized fish balls.

In a small bowl, mix together the panko breadcrumbs with the extra-virgin olive oil. Season with sea salt and black pepper to taste. In another small bowl, whisk the egg whites until lightly foamy.

Dip each fish ball gently in the whisked egg whites, then roll it in the prepared panko breadcrumbs until fully coated. Repeat the process with the remaining fish balls.

Cover a baking tray with parchment paper and spray with a little extra-virgin olive oil. Arrange the fish balls on the tray and spray with little more extra-virgin olive oil.

Bake in the oven for about 5 minutes, then gently roll them on the other side and bake for 5 minutes. To make the fish balls crispier and darker on top, change the oven setting to broil and bake for 3 to 5 minutes.

While the fish balls bake in the oven, prepare the yogurt dip. In a small bowl, mix together the yogurt, lemon zest and garlic, and season with sea salt and black pepper to taste. Refrigerate until ready to serve.

Remove the fish balls from the oven and serve immediately with the yogurt dip on the side.

One-Tray Prosciutto-Wrapped Cod Fillets with Tomatoes

  Dairy-Free, Gluten-Free

This recipe is inspired by the place where I grew up, my beloved Sicily. Although this is not a specifically traditional Sicilian recipe, it definitely showcases some of the region's staple ingredients: fresh cod, cherry tomatoes—Pachino tomatoes are the best!—and fresh aromatic herbs such as oregano and basil leaves. In typical Sicilian fashion, this recipe calls for just a few simple ingredients, so the key to getting it right is choosing the best versions of those ingredients you can find.

My favorite bit of this awesome recipe is that it can all be made on one tray. No fuss, no multiple pans required: only a bowl to season the tomatoes and a baking tray where you can arrange all the ingredients. Simple, easy, quick!

Serves 4

4 (3-oz [80-g]) skinless cod fillets

4 thin slices Parma prosciutto

6 tbsp (90 ml) extra-virgin olive oil, divided

10½ oz (300 g) vine-ripened cherry tomatoes

1 tsp balsamic vinegar

1 clove garlic, grated

A pinch of brown or raw sugar

½ tsp freshly dried oregano leaves

Handful of fresh basil leaves (optional)

Sea salt and freshly cracked black pepper

Preheat the oven to 360° F (180°C, or gas mark 5).

Pat the fish fillets dry with paper towels, then wrap each fillet tightly with a slice of prosciutto. Brush each fillet with 1 tablespoon (15 ml) of extra-virgin olive oil then place them on a baking tray.

In a bowl, mix together the tomatoes with 2 tablespoons (30 ml) of extra-virgin olive oil followed by the balsamic vinegar, garlic, a pinch of sugar, oregano and basil leaves (if using). Season with sea salt and black pepper to taste, and gently mix the ingredients until combined.

Arrange the tomatoes on the tray, pouring any remaining dressing over them.

Place the tray in the oven on the middle shelf, and bake for 10 minutes or until the fish is opaque and cooked through. It should flake easily.

Remove the fish fillets from the oven, and set them aside on a warm plate. Move the tray to the top shelf and continue to cook the tomatoes for 4 to 5 minutes.

Remove the tomatoes from the oven and divide them among plates. Arrange the fish fillets on top and season with black pepper if desired.

Tip: *You can substitute cod fillets with sea bass, monkfish or another meaty white-fleshed fish of your choice.*

Pesce all'Acqua Pazza
(Fish in Crazy Water)

  Dairy-Free, Gluten-Free

First of all, don't be scared. Crazy water is not some sort of angry and moody water you don't want to deal with. The Italian term *acqua pazza* translates to "crazy water." It is used in traditional cuisine to refer to a lightly aromatic tomato broth where any kind of white fish is poached to perfection.

Whenever I find fresh sustainable white fish at the local market, pesce all'acqua pazza is the first recipe that jumps to my mind. Loaded with vibrant flavors ready to explode in your mouth, each and every bite of this dish reminds me of the beautiful summers in Sicily.

Serves 4

4 tbsp (60 ml) extra-virgin olive oil

3 large cloves garlic, grated

⅛ tsp dried red chili flakes, or more to taste

12 oz (350 g) ripe Piccadilly or cherry tomatoes, halved

½ cup (120 ml) hot water

1 tsp fresh thyme leaves

5 fl oz (150 ml) good-quality dry white wine

Sea salt and freshly cracked black pepper

4 (4½-oz [125-g]) white fish fillets, or 2 (12-oz [350-g]) whole fish (such as royal bream, cod, sea bass or red mullet), scaled and cleaned through

Handful of mixed fresh aromatic herbs (parsley, oregano, fennel tops, thyme)

1 lemon, cut into wedges

Heat the extra-virgin olive oil in a large sauté pan over medium heat. Add the garlic and chili flakes, and cook, stirring often, until the garlic just begins to turn golden, about 30 seconds.

Fold in the tomatoes, water and thyme leaves. Cover with a lid and allow to cook, stirring occasionally, for about 10 minutes. Pour in the wine and cook for another minute, just until the alcohol evaporates.

Taste the tomato sauce, and season accordingly with sea salt and black pepper. Then, with the help of a spatula, push the tomatoes to the edges of the pan.

Place the fish skin-side down in the tomato mixture. Season with a pinch of salt, then cover and cook for about 4 minutes, or until the fish is opaque throughout.

When the fish is ready, remove the fillets with a spatula and divide among four plates. Pour a ladle of the tomato broth on each fillet, top with herbs and serve with a lemon wedge on the side.

Tip: *Use any kind of white fish you like, whether you go for a whole fish (make sure it is scaled and cleaned through) or fish fillets (with skin on for extra flavor). A few of my favorite options include sea bream, cod, red mullet and sea bass.*

Grilled Squid
with Salmoriglio Dressing

  Dairy-Free, Gluten-Free

Grilled squid is one of the simplest and most incredible summertime dishes in Italy. I like to drizzle this quick-to-prepare meal with flavor-packed salmoriglio. If you haven't heard of it before, *salmoriglio* is a classic Sicilian sauce made with extra-virgin olive oil, garlic, lemon and a few herbs. It's used to dress up grilled meat and fish. Once you try it, you'll want to put it on pretty much anything!

Serves 4

1 lb (450 g) whole cleaned squid bodies

4 tbsp (60 ml) extra-virgin olive oil, divided

Juice of 1 lemon

Handful of fresh parsley, finely chopped

½ tbsp (2 g) freshly dried oregano leaves

1 clove garlic, finely minced

Sea salt and freshly cracked black pepper

Heat a large grilling pan over high heat.

Pat the squid bodies dry with paper towels, then brush them with 1 tablespoon (15 ml) of extra-virgin olive oil.

Grill the squids over the hottest part of the grill for 2 to 3 minutes, turning them halfway through the cooking time, until they're browned on both sides.

In a small bowl, whisk together the remaining 3 tablespoons (45 ml) of extra-virgin olive oil with the lemon juice, then fold in the parsley, oregano and garlic. Mix all the ingredients together.

Transfer the grilled squids to a platter, and season them with sea salt and black pepper. Drizzle the prepared salmoriglio all over the squids.

Tip: *Also try salmoriglio with grilled fish or grilled chicken breast to elevate their delicate flavor.*

Braised Cuttlefish with Peas

  Dairy-Free, Gluten-Free

This is such a simple yet lovely traditional Italian way to use cuttlefish. It is quickly braised with crunchy fresh peas and served as a light main. It's not always easy to find fresh or frozen cuttlefish, so feel free to substitute it with squid.

Serves 4

3 tbsp (45 ml) extra-virgin olive oil, divided

28 oz (800 g) cuttlefish, cleaned and cut into ½-inch (1-cm) strips

Sea salt and freshly cracked black pepper

1 shallot

½ clove garlic

A pinch of dried chili flakes

¼ cup (60 ml) white wine

½ cup (120 ml) vegetable or fish stock

1 lb (450 g) fresh or defrosted peas

6–8 fresh mint leaves, finely chopped, for garnish

Heat 2 tablespoons (30 ml) of olive oil in a frying pan over medium-high heat. Toss in the cuttlefish. Stir-fry it for 2 to 3 minutes or until lightly browned. Season with sea salt and black pepper to taste, then remove it from the pan and set it aside, covered.

Reduce the heat to medium and add the remaining 1 tablespoon (15 ml) of extra-virgin olive oil to the pan, followed by the shallot. Cook for 2 to 3 minutes, adding a little water if it browns too much. Stir in the garlic and chili flakes, and cook for another minute.

Return the cuttlefish to the pan, pour in the wine and when it has been absorbed, pour in the stock.

Cover the pan with a lid and cook for 10 minutes over medium-low heat. Add in the peas, and cook all the ingredients for 3 to 4 minutes, or until both the cuttlefish and peas are tender and cooked through. Season with sea salt and black pepper to taste. Remove the pan from the heat, and discard the garlic. Top the cuttlefish and peas with mint leaves, and serve immediately.

Tip: *For a balanced meal, I like to serve this cuttlefish with peas with a large green salad and some steamed or roasted new potatoes on the side.*

Pulses & Grains Ready in Less than 20 Minutes

If you think pulses and grains are super boring or take too much time to cook, I'm here to prove you wrong! They are a favorite in our family. We usually don't eat a large amount of meat during the week, so in order to fuel us with protein, I always try to make fun, creative dishes using nutrient-packed grains and legumes.

With a few tricks and traditional Italian cuisine as inspiration, you can get my Dad's Super-Fast Pasta & Fagioli (page 117) or a comforting bowl of Hearty Chickpea & Potato Soup (page 114) on the table in 20 minutes or less. Venture into perfect springtime dishes like a nutrient-loaded vegan frittata (page 125), or try out-of-the-box ingredient combinations for a refreshing summer meal—my Barley, Pea & Ricotta Bowl (page 113) is a MUST!

And if you're in a hurry, take a look at my 10-Minute Seafood Couscous (page 121). It feeds a village and is always a winner!

Barley, Pea & Ricotta Bowl

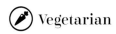 Vegetarian

Ricotta and peas go so well together and are such a classic Italian combo. They are often found together in pasta, but barley makes a great nutritious alternative. It's loaded with lovely nutty flavor and al dente texture and gives an interesting twist to traditional dishes.

This bowl brings together crunchy peas, sweet ricotta, refreshing basil and zesty lemon for a hearty and super quick meal. It kind of reminds me of a risotto, but it's much simpler and more forgiving to make!

Serves 4

1 cup (200 g) pearled barley, rinsed

Sea salt

2 tbsp + 1 tsp (30 ml + 5 ml) extra-virgin olive oil, divided (plus more for serving, optional)

1 small shallot, finely minced

1 clove garlic

A pinch of dried red chili flakes

1 cup (130 g) fresh or defrosted peas

4–5 basil leaves, chopped

½ cup (120 g) fresh ricotta cheese, drained

Zest of 1 lemon

Freshly cracked black pepper

Bring a large pot of water to a boil. Add the barley, season with sea salt and simmer, stirring occasionally, until the barley is cooked through but still chewy, about 15 minutes.

Heat 2 tablespoons (30 ml) of extra-virgin olive oil in a frying pan over medium heat. Add the shallot, and cook for 2 to 3 minutes, adding a little water if it browns too much. Toss in the garlic and chili flakes, and cook for another minute.

Stir the peas into the pan and cook for 4 to 5 minutes, stirring occasionally, until the peas are tender but still crunchy, then discard the garlic.

Drain the barley, and transfer it into the pan with the peas. Add the basil leaves, stir to combine all the ingredients and remove the pan from the heat.

Place the ricotta and lemon zest in a small bowl. Drizzle with 1 teaspoon of extra-virgin olive oil, and season with sea salt and black pepper to taste. Gently whisk all the ingredients together.

Divide the barley and peas among four bowls. Top with dollops of the ricotta mixture, and drizzle with more extra-virgin olive oil if desired.

Tip: *Feel free to add a couple of tablespoons of my Broccoli Pesto (page 47) or Homemade Basil Pesto (page 35) if you have any leftovers in the fridge!*

Hearty Chickpea & Potato Soup

 Vegan

This nourishing soup works amazingly well with different kinds of grains. I like to add barley or farro for a hearty flavor, but pasta or rice would work well too. This cozy soup is naturally vegan, but if you don't have any particular dietary restrictions, try it topped with Pecorino Romano shavings for a nice kick of flavor.

Serves 4

3 tbsp (45 ml) extra-virgin olive oil, divided

1 medium yellow or white onion, chopped

1 carrot, peeled and finely minced

2 lb (900 g) potatoes, peeled and finely cubed

2 tbsp (3 g) rosemary leaves, finely chopped

Sea salt and freshly cracked black pepper

4 cups (1 L) vegetable stock

7 oz (200 g) short pasta (such as ditali or mezzi rigatoni) or other grain of choice

2 (10-oz [280-g]) jars of chickpeas, drained

Heat 2 tablespoons (30 ml) of extra-virgin olive oil in a large pot over medium-high heat. Add the onion, carrot and potatoes, followed by the rosemary leaves. Sauté the ingredients for 5 minutes or until the vegetables begin to soften. Season with sea salt and black pepper to taste.

Pour in the stock, cover the pot with a lid and simmer for 7 minutes. Fold in the pasta and chickpeas, and season with sea salt and black pepper. Cook until the pasta is done and the potatoes are tender.

Remove the pot from the heat. Divide the chickpea and potato soup among four bowls, drizzle with the remaining extra-virgin olive oil and top with black pepper just before serving.

Dad's Super-Fast Pasta & Fagioli

On a cold and rainy day, *pasta e fagioli* is the hearty, comforting meal that jumps to my mind. My dad loved this dish, and he would usually whip up a super-fast version after a tiring day at the office. I absolutely loved it too, and I've learned a few of his tricks over the years. The main secret for his pasta e fagioli is a jar of borlotti beans. Traditional pasta e fagioli requires dry borlotti beans, a little organization and longer prep time, so if you don't have any of those, this is the right pasta e fagioli for you. After many years, this recipe still amazes me! You could never tell it's made with bottled or canned beans rather than dry beans, and it looks like you have spent hours on it instead of just fifteen minutes!

Serves 4

3 tbsp (45 ml) extra-virgin olive oil, divided

1 shallot, finely minced

2 thin slices Parma prosciutto, roughly chopped

2 (10-oz [280-g]) jars of borlotti beans, drained

2 sage leaves, finely chopped

1 tsp rosemary leaves, finely chopped

4 cups (1 L) hot vegetable stock, divided

12 oz (350 g) short pasta, such as ditali or mezzi rigatoni

4 tbsp (22 g) grated Parmesan cheese, for garnish

Freshly cracked black pepper

Heat 2 tablespoons (30 ml) of extra-virgin olive in a large pan over medium-low heat. Add the shallot and cook until it begins to turn golden, adding a bit of warm water if necessary.

Add the prosciutto to the pan and sauté for 2 minutes over medium-high heat, or until crispy. Then add the borlotti beans, sage and rosemary leaves, pour in half the stock and simmer for 5 minutes, stirring occasionally.

Remove half of the bean soup mixture, blend it until smooth and return it to the pot. Pour the remaining stock into the pot, and add the pasta. Cook, stirring occasionally, until the pasta is done.

Divide the pasta e fagioli among four bowls. Top with Parmesan cheese and black pepper, and drizzle with the remaining extra-virgin olive oil.

Tip: *Choose borlotti beans sold in glass jars over canned beans whenever possible. They taste so much better!*

Nourishing Farro, Chickpea & Grilled Vegetables

 Vegetarian

Farro is a nutritious grain. If this is your first time working with farro, don't panic! This grain is incredibly easy to make and remains al dente even if slightly over-cooked. It's chewy, hearty and filling with a slightly nutty flavor, making it an interesting alternative to pasta and rice. It works great tossed into soups and salads, and I especially love it paired with flavorsome grilled veggies, chickpeas and a vibrant Italian lemon vinaigrette for a light, filling lunch.

Serves 4

8 oz (230 g) Italian farro

2 zucchini, sliced diagonally ½-inch (1-cm) thick

1 red onion, sliced ½-inch (1-cm) thick

1 large beefsteak tomato, sliced ½-inch (1-cm) thick

1 large eggplant, sliced ½-inch (1-cm) thick

4 tbsp (60 ml) extra-virgin olive oil

Sea salt and freshly cracked black pepper

1½ cups (240 g) cooked chickpeas, rinsed

Handful of basil leaves, torn

For the Dressing

2 tbsp (30 ml) extra-virgin olive oil

Juice of 1 lemon

1 tsp good-quality honey

1 tsp freshly dried oregano leaves

Sea salt and freshly cracked black pepper

Bring a pot of lightly salted water to a boil. Place the farro in a fine-mesh sieve and rinse well with cold water. Drain the farro, place it in the boiling water and cook for about 15 minutes, or until the farro is just tender.

Heat a large grilling pan over medium-high heat. Brush the zucchini, onion, tomato and eggplant with the extra-virgin olive oil. Season with sea salt and black pepper to taste. Grill the vegetables over medium-high heat, turning them occasionally, until lightly charred and tender, 15 minutes.

While the farro and vegetables cook, prepare the dressing. In a small bowl, whisk together the extra-virgin olive oil, the lemon juice, honey and oregano. Season with sea salt and black pepper to taste, and set aside until needed.

Drain and quickly rinse the farro under running water to cool it slightly, then transfer it to a large bowl. Pour the dressing all over the farro, and toss to combine well.

Transfer the grilled vegetables to a chopping board and cut them into bite-sized pieces.

Add the grilled vegetables, chickpeas and basil leaves to the bowl with the farro, and toss all the ingredients together.

Tip: *This salad will keep well for up to a couple of days in the refrigerator. For extra flavor, you can substitute the water with stock when cooking the farro. If you're a major cheese lover, feel free to add a dollop or two of ricotta cheese, or top the salad with a whole fresh burrata or buffalo mozzarella ball.*

10-Minute Seafood Couscous to Feed a Crowd

 Dairy-Free

Need a fast, tasty meal to feed a large crowd? This couscous appetizer feeds up to eight people, and it's just perfect to share.

Inspired by a traditional Sicilian recipe—*Couscous alla Trapanese*—this quick version is loaded with flavor but ready in a fraction of the time, so you have more time to chat and mingle!

Serves 4 to 6

2 tbsp (30 ml) extra-virgin olive oil, divided

1 clove garlic

1 lb (450 g) fresh mussels, scrubbed and cleaned

½ cup (120 ml) white wine

14 oz (400 g) fresh calamari, cleaned and cut into rings

Handful of cherry tomatoes, halved and deseeded

8 fresh shrimp, cleaned

1 tsp double-concentrated tomato paste

2 tbsp (30 ml) warm water

Sea salt and freshly cracked black pepper

7 oz (200 g) couscous (uncooked)

A pinch of saffron

1 cup (240 ml) hot fish or vegetable stock

1 tbsp (3 g) fresh parsley leaves, finely chopped

Heat 1 tablespoon (15 ml) of extra-virgin olive oil and the garlic in a large pot over medium-high heat. Add the mussels, followed by the white wine, and sauté them for 2 minutes. Cover the pot with a lid and simmer until the mussels open, about 2 minutes. Discard the garlic clove and the mussels that did not open, then pour their juice through a sieve. Set both the cooked mussels and their filtered juice aside.

Return the pan to the heat with 1 tablespoon (15 ml) of extra-virgin olive oil. Add the calamari and tomatoes, and sauté them for 2 minutes. Fold in the shrimp, then pour in the mussel juice, the tomato paste and 2 tablespoons (30 ml) of warm water. Continue to cook all the ingredients for 4 to 5 minutes. Add the mussels back to the pan, season with salt and pepper to taste and remove from the heat.

Place the couscous in a large bowl. Sprinkle a pinch of saffron into the stock, and pour it over the couscous. Cover the bowl and let it sit undisturbed for about 5 minutes, or until the couscous is cooked through. Fluff the couscous lightly with a fork, and transfer it to a large serving plate. Pour the seafood sauce over the couscous, and sprinkle the parsley on top.

Chickpea Crespelle (Chickpea Pancakes)

Gluten-Free

Crespelle are basically the Italian version of French crêpes, and they are usually served with savory ingredients. These chickpea crespelle are one of my favorite variations, because they're super nutritious and much easier to make than crêpes, plus they're totally egg-free, gluten-free, dairy-free and vegan.

Feel free to fill them with pretty much anything you like. I love to serve mine with a classic combo of goat cheese, arugula and cherry tomatoes in summertime, or with some sautéed spinach and mushrooms during the winter.

Serves 4

1 cup (100 g) chickpea flour

7 fl oz (200 ml) cold water

1 tbsp (15 ml) extra-virgin olive oil, plus more for greasing

½ tsp sea salt and freshly cracked black pepper, to taste

To Serve

Handful of arugula leaves

Handful of cherry tomatoes, chopped

7 oz (200 g) fresh goat cheese

Place the chickpea flour in a large bowl, and slowly whisk in the water until fully incorporated. Whisk in the extra-virgin olive oil, and season with sea salt and black pepper to taste. Whisk gently to combine all the ingredients, until the batter has reached a lump-free velvety consistency. Cover the bowl with plastic wrap and refrigerate for 5 minutes.

Heat a 10-inch (26-cm) crêpe pan over medium-high heat. Drizzle it with extra-virgin olive oil and use a paper towel to grease the whole pan surface.

Add a ladle-full of mixture to the pan and shake gently to spread it around, adding more mixture if needed to fully cover the base of the pan. Cook for approximately 4 minutes, then gently flip over and cook on the other side until golden brown, about 2 minutes. Repeat the process with the remaining chickpea mixture.

Transfer the chickpea crespelle to a plate. Serve filled with arugula, tomatoes and fresh goat cheese. Alternatively, fill them with your favorite fillings.

Super-Nutritious, Vegan Chickpea Frittata with Greens

  Gluten-Free, Vegan

When I had my first bite of a chickpea frittata, I was totally impressed. It had a similar texture and taste to a classic frittata, but no eggs or cheese were involved!

This chickpea frittata is inspired by an Italian classic called *farinata di ceci* (chickpea farinata) which can be easily mistaken for a classic frittata. Farinata di ceci is typically thin, crispy and served on its own, but in an attempt to liven up this traditional dish, I combined the basic recipe with some of my favorite greens, *et voilà*, this vegan, super-nutritious chickpea frittata was born.

Serves 4

2 cups (200 g) chickpea flour

10 fl oz (300 ml) cold water

3 tbsp (45 ml) extra-virgin olive oil, divided

Sea salt and freshly cracked black pepper

1 leek, finely sliced

5 oz (150 g) fresh kale, de-stemmed and chopped

½ cup (120 ml) warm water

5 oz (150 g) fresh baby spinach leaves

Place the chickpea flour in a large bowl, and slowly whisk in the water until fully incorporated. Whisk in 1 tablespoon (15 ml) of extra-virgin olive oil. Season with sea salt and black pepper to taste. Whisk gently to combine all the ingredients, until the batter has reached a lump-free, velvety consistency. Cover the bowl with plastic wrap and refrigerate for 5 minutes.

Heat 1 tablespoon (15 ml) of extra-virgin olive oil in a large frying pan over medium heat, then fold in the chopped leek and kale and stir-fry for 1 to 2 minutes. Pour in ½ cup (120 ml) of warm water, cover with a lid and cook for 3 minutes, until it boils down. Add in the spinach leaves, cover again with a lid and continue to cook until the vegetables have softened, about 2 minutes. Season with sea salt and black pepper to taste.

Pour 1 tablespoon (15 ml) of extra-virgin olive oil into the pan and distribute the veggies evenly over the surface of the pan. Pour in the prepared chickpea mixture, making sure to evenly cover the veggies, cover with a lid and cook over low heat for 8 to 10 minutes.

The frittata is ready when it is easily pulled off the bottom and has reached a dense consistency. Remove the pan from the heat, and carefully slide the frittata onto a serving plate.

Sautéed Tuscan Kale with Pumpkin & Cannellini Beans

  Gluten-Free, Vegan

Tuscan kale or *cavolo nero* has always been a staple ingredient in the Italian cuisine, and it's the star of the popular Tuscan soup called *ribollita*. Inspired by this traditional soup, I put together this heart-warming kale, pumpkin and cannellini beans dish, which echoes ribollita in flavor but takes a fraction of the time to prepare. Served with crusty bread, it makes a feel-good vegan meal on its own. It also can be easily served as a hearty side to go along with a wintery dish such as my Quick Lemon Chicken Piccata (page 77).

Serves 4

3 tbsp (45 ml) extra-virgin olive oil, divided

1 medium yellow or white onion, chopped

2 sprigs of thyme

½ tsp red chili pepper flakes

7 oz (200 g) pumpkin flesh, finely cubed

10½ oz (300 g) Tuscan kale, roughly chopped

Sea salt and freshly cracked black pepper

1 cup (240 ml) vegetable stock

1 (13-oz [370-g]) jar of cannellini beans

Crusty bread, for serving (optional)

Heat 2 tablespoons (30 ml) of extra-virgin olive oil in a large pot over medium-high heat. Add the onion, thyme sprigs and chili flakes, followed by the pumpkin and kale. Sauté the ingredients for 5 minutes or until the vegetables begin to soften. Season with sea salt and black pepper to taste.

Pour in the stock, cover the pot with a lid and simmer for 5 minutes. Fold in the cannellini beans and cook for 5 minutes, or until the vegetables are cooked through.

Remove the pot from the heat, drizzle with 1 tablespoon (15 ml) of extra-virgin olive oil and season with black pepper. Divide among four bowls, and serve with crusty bread, if desired.

Speedy Nutritious Salads

What's not to love about Italian salads? Offering endless texture and flavor combinations to play with, they make your taste buds rejoice. And you can make them with minimal effort!

Growing up, my mum would always put a big, colorful and never-boring salad on our dinner table, so my brothers and I were and still are major salads eaters. At the big annual family gatherings, my mother-in-law still gets amusingly surprised by the mammoth amount of salad my part of the family devours!

So, long story short, I love salads, and I try to make them as fun, creative and nutritious as possible by making the most of seasonal ingredients and drawing inspiration from the vast array of flavors traditional Italian cuisine offers.

In this chapter, you'll find the recipes we eat at home on repeat! They're all packed with bold, refreshing flavors and simple ingredients in typical Italian fashion, and they're perfect to eat on their own or served with your favorite mains.

Nutrient-Packed Chickpea Panzanella

 Vegan

Panzanella is one of my favorite summer dishes, and it tastes so good that I had to share not one but two recipes with you in this book. This version features crunchy nutritious chickpeas and makes a wonderful speedy and satisfying lunch the whole family will love.

Serves 4

3 thick slices artisanal ciabatta bread

½ clove garlic

5 tbsp (75 ml) fruity extra-virgin olive oil, divided

1 small red onion

½ large cucumber, seeds removed

12 oz (350 g) cherry tomatoes

1 tsp freshly dried Italian oregano leaves

Handful of fresh basil and mint leaves

1 (8-oz [230-g]) glass jar of cooked chickpeas, drained

Sea salt and freshly cracked black pepper

Rub each side of the bread slices with the garlic clove.

Cut the bread into ½-inch (1-cm) cubes, and place them in a large bowl. Drizzle with 1 tablespoon (15 ml) of extra-virgin olive oil, and combine all the ingredients together.

Heat a large grilling pan over medium heat, then add the bread cubes and grill until nicely golden brown and crisp on each side, about 5 minutes. Remove the bread, and set it aside to cool.

Finely slice the onion, finely chop the cucumber into small cubes and roughly chop the tomatoes. Add all the ingredients into the same bowl used to season the bread cubes.

Toss the remaining 4 tablespoons (60 ml) of extra-virgin olive oil, oregano leaves, basil and mint leaves and the drained chickpeas into the bowl. Season with sea salt and black pepper to taste.

Fold in the toasted bread cubes, and stir to combine all the ingredients.

Vibrant Mint & Zucchini Farro Salad

 Vegan

This refreshing summer salad comes together in a blink with basically zero effort. It features refreshing zucchini tossed with hearty farro, fresh mint, tangy lemon and a swirl of fruity extra-virgin olive oil. If you're looking for a vibrant salad that's packed with different flavors and textures, this is the one. And it also happens to be vegan, so it's perfect to bring to summer get-togethers!

Serves 4

1⅔ cups (230 g) Italian farro

2 medium zucchini (or 4 baby zucchini), deseeded and finely cubed

Handful of mint leaves, finely chopped

Zest of 1 lemon

4 tbsp (60 ml) good-quality extra-virgin olive oil

Sea salt and freshly cracked black pepper

Bring a pot of lightly salted water to a boil. Place the farro in a fine-mesh sieve and rinse well with cold water. Drain the farro, place it in the boiling water and cook for about 15 minutes, or until the farro is just tender.

In a large bowl, combine the finely cubed zucchini, mint leaves and lemon zest. Drizzle with the extra-virgin olive oil, and season with sea salt and black pepper to taste.

Drain and quickly rinse the farro under running water to cool it slightly, then transfer it to the bowl with the marinated zucchini. Toss to combine all the ingredients together.

Tip: *If you can, opt for fresh baby zucchini, which have a sweeter note than classic zucchini and work amazingly well in this recipe. If you can't find farro, substitute with barley or couscous.*

10-Minute Mediterranean Couscous Salad

Vegan (if using vegetable broth)

This salad is super easy, nutritious and ready in less than ten minutes! I could eat this on repeat, no matter the season and the weather. It's hearty, satisfying and packed with lots of fresh veggies—not to mention so easy you could make it blindfolded. This salad makes a lovely meal on its own, but it's just as great served as a side dish. My secret ingredient, which brings this salad to the next level, is my mum's freshly dried oregano sent over directly from Sicily. Since I imagine most of you aren't lucky enough to have family living in Italy, you can easily replicate my secret ingredient at your local grocery store by choosing dried oregano sold in bunches instead of the oregano sold in jars. You will thank me later.

Serves 4

1¼ cups (200 g) couscous (uncooked)

Sea salt and freshly cracked black pepper

1 cup (240 ml) hot chicken or vegetable broth

1 tbsp (15 ml) fresh lemon juice

2 tbsp (30 ml) extra-virgin olive oil

1 clove garlic, grated

1 (15-oz [425-g]) can chickpeas, rinsed and drained

5 oz (150 g) cherry tomatoes, halved

1 large cucumber, diced

½ red onion, finely sliced

Handful of fresh arugula

1 tsp freshly dried oregano leaves

1 tbsp (3 g) fresh basil leaves, chopped

1 tbsp (3 g) fresh mint leaves, chopped

In a medium bowl, add the couscous and season it with sea salt and black pepper to taste. Pour the broth over the couscous, cover with a lid and let it stand for about 5 minutes, or until the couscous is cooked through. Allow it to cool for a couple of minutes.

In a small jar, add the lemon juice, extra-virgin olive oil and garlic. Close the lid and shake well, until all the ingredients are combined.

Place the prepared couscous in a large bowl and fluff it up with the help of a fork. Fold in the chickpeas, tomatoes, cucumber, onion, arugula, oregano, basil and mint leaves. Pour the prepared dressing all over the salad, then toss everything together. Season with sea salt and black pepper to taste.

Tip: *Brighten up the salad with other Italian staple ingredients. Some of my favorites include jar-preserved tuna fillets, sun-dried tomatoes, Nocellara olives, burrata or mozzarella cheese.*

Sicilian Orange & Fennel Salad

  Gluten-Free, Vegan

This fresh, fruity salad is a staple of Sicilian cuisine. We love to eat it as a side for grilled fish, but it works just as amazingly with poultry and meat, or simply on its own for a refreshing light lunch. This salad is one of my favorite things to eat when fresh juicy oranges are in season—their sweet and tangy flavor pairs beautifully with bittersweet black olives and the refreshing licorice-like flavor of the fennel. Don't forget to drizzle your salad with the orange vinaigrette—it adds such a refreshing note!

Serves 4

For the Orange Vinaigrette

1 tbsp (9 g) red onion, finely diced

½ tsp orange zest

1 tbsp (15 ml) white wine vinegar

2 tbsp (30 ml) fresh orange juice

2 tbsp (30 ml) extra-virgin olive oil

½ tsp sea salt and freshly cracked black pepper, to taste

For the Salad

4 large blood or navel oranges (I recommend organic)

3 fennel bulbs, finely sliced

Handful of arugula leaves

1 small red onion, finely sliced

½ tbsp (1 g) freshly dried Italian oregano

Handful of black olives

To make the orange vinaigrette, combine the onion and orange zest in a small bowl. Pour in the white wine vinegar, orange juice and extra-virgin olive oil. Season with sea salt and black pepper to taste, and toss all the ingredients to combine. Set the vinaigrette aside until needed.

To prepare the salad, start by segmenting the oranges. Cut the top and the bottom of each orange, then slice off the peel and white membrane and then gently cut the oranges into thick slices horizontally.

Place the orange slices in a large bowl, and fold in the fennel, arugula leaves, red onion, oregano and black olives. Toss all the ingredients to combine.

Pour the orange vinaigrette over the orange and fennel salad, toss gently to combine the ingredients and adjust the seasoning.

Tuscan-Style Cannellini Beans & Shrimp Salad

  Dairy-Free, Gluten-Free

A simple yet delectable salad that combines sweet cannellini beans and grilled shrimp for an elegant salad you can serve for a last-minute dinner party or a quick summer lunch.

I love how simple this salad is to prepare, as long as you have some cannellini beans in your pantry and a bag of frozen shrimp in your freezer—but try to go fresh for best flavors! This dish can be thrown together in mere minutes and is guaranteed to please the most refined palates.

Serves 4

½ lb (235 g) fresh large shrimps (or frozen)

2 tbsp (30 ml) extra-virgin olive oil, divided

1 clove garlic, minced

Sea salt and freshly cracked black pepper

1 (13-oz [370-g]) jar of cannellini beans

1 red onion, finely sliced

Juice and zest of 1 lemon

Handful of basil leaves

Pull off the head of each shrimp and discard it. Using a small paring knife, cut along the outer edge of the shrimp's back, about ¼ inch (6 mm) deep. Remove and discard the vein that runs on the back using your fingers or the tip of the knife.

Heat 1 tablespoon (15 ml) of extra-virgin olive oil and the garlic in a large frying pan over medium heat. Add the shrimp and cook, stirring often, for about 5 minutes, or until the shrimp is pink, opaque and cooked through. Season with sea salt and black pepper to taste. Remove the pan from the heat, and allow the shrimp to cool slightly.

In a large bowl, place the cannellini beans, red onion, lemon juice and zest and the remaining 1 tablespoon (15 ml) of extra-virgin olive oil. Fold in the cooked shrimps and basil leaves, and mix all the ingredients gently until combined.

Melon, Zucchini, Prosciutto & Stracciatella Salad

🌾 Gluten-Free

This is such a simple salad to prepare, and it is absolutely delicious. The creamy stracciatella cheese may be best known as the delicious center of burrata, and it pairs simply beautifully with sweet cantaloupe and salty prosciutto. Add mint leaves and crunchy zucchini ribbons for a refreshing twist. Serve it on its own or with roasted chicken, grilled fish or a healthy grain of your choice.

Serves 4

2 medium zucchini

1 cantaloupe, peeled and sliced

1 tbsp (3 g) fresh mint leaves

2 tbsp (30 ml) extra-virgin olive oil, plus more for serving

Sea salt and freshly cracked black pepper

6 slices Prosciutto di Parma

7 oz (200 g) fresh stracciatella or burrata cheese

Using a peeler, cut the zucchini into thin slices, and place it in a large bowl with water and ice.

Drain the zucchini slices and pat them dry with paper towels, then transfer them to a large bowl. Mix in the cantaloupe slices and mint leaves, then season with the extra-virgin olive oil, and sea salt and black pepper to taste.

Arrange the salad on a large serving plate. Take a slice of prosciutto and wrap it around itself to form a small rose. Repeat the process with the remaining slices, and place the prosciutto roses on top of the salad.

Scatter spoonfuls of stracciatella cheese over the salad, and drizzle lightly with extra-virgin olive oil.

Tip: *For more adventurous flavors, substitute stracciatella or burrata with small chunks of hard cheese, such as Pecorino Romano or Parmesan cheese.*

Winter Persimmon
& Pomegranate Salad

  Dairy-Free, Gluten-Free, Vegetarian

This salad makes the most of two of my favorite winter superfoods: persimmon and pomegranate, both loaded with powerful nutritional value!

I like to use crisp persimmons when making this salad—Fuyu or slightly ripe Hachiya varieties are the best. This fruit, although not strictly a traditional Italian ingredient, has been consistently gaining popularity over the years, and my family loves it. This salad is divine in its simplicity, so I often serve it on its own. It also pairs wonderfully with Italian fresh cheeses, such as ricotta, mascarpone and burrata, or aged ones, such as Parmesan or Pecorino Romano.

Serves 4

3 firm Fuyu persimmons, peeled

5 oz (150 g) baby salad leaves

2 tbsp (30 ml) extra-virgin olive oil

1 tsp honey

Fleur de sel or sea salt flakes and freshly cracked black pepper

½ cup (75 g) pomegranate seeds

⅔ cup (75 g) toasted pistachios, finely chopped, for garnish

Slice off the tops and bottoms of the persimmons, then cut them horizontally into thin slices. Transfer them to a large bowl, and add in the baby salad leaves, extra-virgin olive oil and honey. Season with salt and pepper to taste. Gently toss all the ingredients to combine.

Transfer the salad to a serving plate, scatter the pomegranate seeds over the top and garnish with the toasted pistachios.

Tip: *If persimmons are unavailable, use Asian pears or Honeycrisp apples.*

Apple, Celery & Walnut Salad with Gorgonzola Sauce

(🌾) Gluten-Free

A highly nutritious, speedy winter salad featuring a classic combo of apple, walnuts and celery, all dressed up with a delicious Gorgonzola cream. If you haven't tried Gorgonzola cheese before, it's the Italian king of blue cheeses. Its sweet and delicately spicy notes make it the perfect cheese to pair with juicy Honeycrisp apples.

Serves 4

½ cup (60 g) Gorgonzola cheese

2 tbsp (30 ml) milk

Handful of baby salad leaves

2 Honeycrisp apples, cored and finely sliced

2 ribs celery, finely chopped or sliced into ribbons

½ cup (60 g) walnuts, chopped

Sea salt flakes and freshly cracked black pepper

Place the Gorgonzola in a bowl, and slowly pour in the milk while whisking, until fully incorporated. Continue to whisk the cheese mixture until it reaches a creamy, dense consistency, then set it aside until needed.

Arrange a bed of baby salad leaves on a serving plate, and scatter the apples, celery and walnuts on top. Drizzle the Gorgonzola sauce all over the salad, and season with sea salt and black pepper to taste.

New Potato, Green Bean & Tuna Salad

  Dairy-Free, Gluten-Free

My mum will be super excited to see one of her favorite dishes in this book. She absolutely adores this salad and makes it on a weekly basis when green beans are in season. She loves to make it with thinly sliced red onion, but I'm a garlic girl, so I've swapped it for a tiny bit of garlic. If you like my mum's version best, go ahead and add that red onion, as long as you let me know. I'll pass on the message, and you'll make her day!

Serves 4

1 lb (450 g) small new potatoes

2 cups (200 g) green beans, trimmed

3 tbsp (45 ml) extra-virgin olive oil

1 clove garlic, grated

5 oz (150 g) tuna fillets in a jar, drained

1 tsp freshly dried oregano leaves

Sea salt and freshly cracked black pepper

Bring a large pot of water to a boil, then add the potatoes and cook for 5 minutes. Add the green beans and continue to cook the vegetables for 5 minutes, or until both are tender.

Drain the vegetables, and transfer them to a large bowl. Pour in the extra-virgin olive oil followed by the garlic, tuna fillets and oregano leaves. Season with sea salt and black pepper to taste, and stir to combine all the ingredients.

Fig, Prosciutto & Burrata Salad

(🌾) Gluten-Free

Every year when fig season starts, this salad is the first thing I make, and it puts me instantly into a summer mood. Fresh figs, arugula, burrata, prosciutto and basil tossed with a lively honey-balsamic vinaigrette make for a fuss-free, perfect-for-summer salad.

Slightly ripe Italian figs work amazingly in this salad—they have a unique, rich texture and a luscious, sweet flavor—but any other variety will do the job just fine. Try to pick organic figs when they're in season. I also recommend getting freshly sliced Parma prosciutto from a local Italian deli rather than buying pre-packaged slices. Last but not least, I love adding burrata cheese into the mix. It's milky, loaded with flavor and wonderfully melts in your mouth.

A few glorious, handpicked ingredients are all you need to turn a simple dish like this into a sophisticated salad to serve at any summer get-together.

Serves 4

8 thin slices Parma prosciutto

2 tbsp (30 ml) extra-virgin olive oil

1 tsp good-quality balsamic vinegar

1 tsp good-quality honey

Fleur de sel or sea salt flakes and freshly cracked black pepper

7 oz (200 g) fresh arugula leaves

8 oz (230 g) fresh burrata cheese

4 fresh figs, quartered

Handful of fresh basil leaves

Take a slice of prosciutto and wrap it around itself to form a small rose. Then repeat the process with the remaining slices, and set the roses aside.

In a small jar, combine the extra-virgin olive oil, balsamic vinegar and honey. Season with sea salt and black pepper to taste, close the lid and shake the jar for a few seconds to combine all the ingredients.

Place the arugula leaves on a serving plate, and arrange the prosciutto roses over the top. Tear the burrata over the top of the salad, scatter with figs and torn basil leaves and drizzle the prepared vinaigrette all over.

Effortless Everyday Sides

Side dishes play a fundamental role at the dinner table. A side dish can enhance the taste of a second dish and accompany it in a harmonious way. They help us feel full, and they balance out our meals, making sure we get all the nutrients that we need to face our day.

Colorful, flavor-packed side dishes always go hand in hand with main courses in Italian cuisine. This culinary tradition offers infinite variations, and it makes the most of simple, inexpensive ingredients and seasonal produce.

In this chapter, I've put together some of the most traditional side dishes that I like to make on a daily basis, including fun ways to serve simple veggies and a super quick version of classic roasted potatoes (page 157) that you'll want to make over and over again!

Quick-Marinated Eggplant Carpaccio

 Gluten-Free, Vegan

This eggplant carpaccio is one of my favorite recipes to make in the summer, when eggplants are juicy and sweet and my grilling pan is out twenty-four hours a day, ready to cook all sorts of delicious foods. This easy starter is delicious served with grilled bread, but it'll work just as great as a side dish to grilled meat or fish.

I like to use a simple mix of fresh mint and basil leaves, but you can choose any of your favorite fresh herbs—they all work great with eggplant.

Serves 4

2 large dark-skinned Italian eggplants

½ cup (120 ml) extra-virgin olive oil, divided

1 clove garlic, grated

1 tbsp (3 g) fresh mint leaves, finely minced

1 tbsp (3 g) fresh basil leaves, finely minced

Juice of 1 lemon

Sea salt and freshly cracked black pepper

Cut off the ends of the eggplants, and slice them into thin ¼-inch (6-mm) strips. Brush both sides of each slice lightly with one-third of the extra-virgin olive oil.

Heat a nonstick grilling skillet over medium-high heat. Add the eggplant in one layer and grill for 2 minutes on each side, or until golden brown on both sides. Remove the eggplant from the skillet, and repeat the process with the remaining slices.

In a small bowl, mix together the remaining extra-virgin olive oil with the garlic, fresh herbs and lemon juice. Then season generously with sea salt and black pepper, and set aside.

Arrange the grilled eggplant slices in a single layer, gently overlapping each other, in a large casserole dish or serving plate. Pour the prepared dressing all over the vegetables. Or, if you have a little more time on hand, cover the eggplant carpaccio and allow it to marinate in the fridge overnight. You'll bite into an exploding-with-flavor starter the next day!

Tip: *If you do a lot of slicing or make this eggplant carpaccio as often as I do, ask Santa for a mandoline this year. After years of risking my thumb with traditional knife slicing, I discovered the beauty of this kitchen tool. The only thing I've cut since is prep time!*

Spring-Perfect Frittata

⊛ Gluten-Free

Nothing screams spring more than a green veggie-loaded frittata. Easy to make, loaded with nutrients and perfect to feed a whole family in minutes, the frittata is probably one of the most loved dishes by Italian families. When I'm trying to get my son to eat as many greens as possible, this frittata works like a charm.

If you're not familiar with Grana Padano cheese, it is the "cousin" of Parmesan cheese. They're very similar and often get confused, but Grana Padano has a milder taste and a tender texture. It works well in this recipe and pairs beautifully with the delicate flavor of the veggies I've used, but you can definitely substitute it with Parmesan cheese if you like.

Serves 4

3½ oz (100 g) fresh green asparagus

3 tbsp (45 ml) extra-virgin olive oil, divided

1 small white onion, finely minced

7 oz (200 g) frozen or fresh peas

½ cup (120 ml) hot vegetable stock or water

Handful of fresh spinach leaves

Sea salt and freshly cracked black pepper

6 fresh large eggs

6 tbsp (33 g) freshly grated Grana Padano cheese

5–6 fresh basil leaves

2 sprigs fresh thyme, leaves only

Scrape the asparagus stalks with a peeler to remove the hardest parts, then finely chop the stems and cut the tips in half.

Heat a large pan over medium heat and drizzle evenly with 2 tablespoons (30 ml) of the extra-virgin olive oil. Add the onion, followed by the peas and the asparagus stalks and tips. Pour the hot stock all over the vegetables and cook until the asparagus are just tender, about 5 minutes, stirring occasionally.

Add the spinach leaves to the pan and continue to cook the greens for 2 minutes. Season with sea salt and black pepper to taste. Remove from the heat and distribute the veggies, evenly covering the bottom of the pan.

In a medium-sized bowl, beat the eggs together with the Grana Padano cheese, and season with sea salt and black pepper. Fold in the basil leaves and thyme and beat all the ingredients until combined.

Return the pan with the vegetables back to medium heat, and drizzle generously with 1 tablespoon (15 ml) of extra-virgin olive oil. Pour in the frittata mixture, cover with a lid and cook for 2 minutes, gently shaking the pan every now and then.

When the frittata is easily pulled off from the bottom, it is ready to be turned. Using a plate with the same diameter as the frittata, carefully put it on top and flip the frittata on the other side, then gently slide it back into the pan.

Cook the frittata on the other side, without the lid, for 5 minutes, then remove from the heat. Carefully slide the frittata onto a serving plate, and cut into wedges.

Speedy Pan-Roasted New Potatoes

Gluten-Free, Vegan

As a proud Italian, I'm totally addicted to roasted new potatoes—without a doubt one of the most popular Italian recipes. This traditional side dish has always been a family favorite. My mum makes these pan-roasted potatoes all the time, served alongside grilled fish or chicken.

My mum loves to keep things simple, so following her path, I like to season my roasted potatoes with a drizzle of high-quality extra-virgin olive oil, garlic, fresh rosemary and freshly dried Sicilian oregano—any other oregano is okay, but opt for the one sold on stems.

Roasted potatoes are awesome and always will be, but sometimes there's just not enough time to cook them in the oven. This crispy skillet version is equally delicious and ready in less than twenty minutes—a total win-win if you ask me!

Serves 4

1 lb (450 g) small new potatoes

3 tbsp (45 ml) extra-virgin olive oil, divided

4 rosemary sprigs, leaves finely minced

4 sage leaves, finely minced

1 tsp freshly dried oregano leaves

Sea salt and freshly cracked black pepper

1 clove garlic

Bring a large pot of water to a boil, then add the potatoes and cook for 7 minutes or until just tender.

Drain the potatoes, and transfer them into a large bowl. Add 2 tablespoons (30 ml) of extra-virgin olive oil followed by the rosemary, sage and oregano leaves. Season with sea salt and black pepper to taste, and stir to combine all the ingredients.

Heat the remaining extra-virgin olive oil together with the garlic in a large skillet over medium heat. Fold in the seasoned potatoes and cook, stirring occasionally, for 5 to 7 minutes, or until crispy outside and moist inside. Discard the garlic from the pan, and season the potatoes with black pepper.

Leftover Spaghetti Frittata

Since I was a kid, my mum has taught me the importance of not wasting food. She is the queen of leftovers, and not a single slice of bread ever goes to waste in our kitchen. Like a real Italian, she prepares pasta every day, which almost always leads to some leftovers. She then uses whatever pasta and sauce is left to make a flavor-packed frittata for the next day. Inspired by her smart way to cut food waste, I try to follow her example. I often like to double my simple Spaghetti alla Carrettiera (page 64) recipe and make this super quick, nutritious frittata the day after.

Use this recipe as a basic canvas and get creative! Make sure to use leftovers with flavors that go well together to guarantee that your frittata will taste amazing. I like to pair cooked ham with peas and spinach or mushrooms with pancetta and kale, but this recipe is my all-time favorite.

Serves 4

2 tbsp (30 ml) extra-virgin olive oil

3 cups (350 g) leftover Spaghetti alla Carrettiera

5 large eggs, beaten

7 tbsp (35 g) grated Parmesan cheese

Handful of spinach leaves, roughly chopped

Sea salt and freshly cracked black pepper

4 mozzarella slices

Preheat the oven to 400°F (200°C).

Heat a medium cast-iron skillet over low heat, and brush it with the extra-virgin olive oil.

In a large bowl, fold in the leftover spaghetti and eggs and mix well. Toss in the Parmesan cheese and spinach leaves, and season with sea salt and black pepper to taste.

Using large tongs, grab the spaghetti from the bowl and gently distribute it evenly over the base of the hot skillet, then pour in the remaining egg-and-veggie mixture.

Cook the frittata over medium heat for about 5 minutes, then top it with the mozzarella slices and transfer the skillet to the oven.

Bake the frittata until the mixture is no longer liquid and it's nicely crispy and golden on top, about 10 minutes.

Remove the frittata from the oven and serve it straight away, or allow it to cool and cut it into slices and serve at room temperature.

Tip: *You can substitute the leftover Spaghetti alla Carrettiera with cooked plain spaghetti and use your favorite fillings or whatever you have left in the fridge. Cooked ham, prosciutto or roasted veggies are some of my go-to ingredients.*

Mushroom & Kale Frittata Crêpes

Gluten–Free

A thinly cooked frittata can be easily transformed into a posh crêpes-look-alike. These frittata crêpes can be served as a side or as an appetizer, but they're nutritious enough to satisfy as a main paired with a large salad. Fill them up with tender kale, earthy wild mushrooms and melt-in-your-mouth Fontina cheese for a hearty fall dish that you'll want to make on repeat.

Serves 4

6 tbsp (90 ml) extra-virgin olive oil, divided

1 small shallot, finely minced

5 oz (150 g) fresh kale, roughly chopped

5 oz (150 g) fresh or defrosted mixed wild mushrooms

A pinch of freshly grated nutmeg

Sea salt and freshly cracked black pepper

6 fresh large eggs

4 tbsp (22 g) freshly grated Parmesan cheese

4 thin slices Fontina cheese

Heat 2 tablespoons (30 ml) of extra-virgin olive oil in a large frying pan over medium heat. Add the shallot, kale and mushrooms. Stir-fry all the ingredients for about 5 minutes, or until the kale is tender and the mushrooms are cooked through. Season with a pinch of nutmeg, and salt and black pepper to taste.

In a medium-sized bowl, beat the eggs together with the Parmesan cheese, and season with sea salt and black pepper.

Heat a small frying pan over medium heat, and grease with 1 tablespoon (15 ml) of extra-virgin olive oil.

Pour a ladleful of egg mixture into the small pan and immediately start swirling it around the pan to get a nice even layer. Allow the thin frittata "crêpe" to cook for 2 minutes, then carefully flip it onto the other side with the help of a large spatula.

Fill the frittata "crêpe" with a couple of spoonfuls of the kale-and-mushroom mixture, top it with 1 slice of Fontina, then fold it in half twice to form a triangle. Remove the frittata from the heat, and transfer it onto a serving plate. Repeat the process with the remaining ingredients, greasing the pan with 1 tablespoon (15 ml) of extra-virgin olive oil each time.

Classic Sautéed Mushrooms

 Gluten-Free, Vegetarian

Classic Italian *funghi trifolati*—which translates to sautéed mushrooms—are a perfect side dish to accompany fall and winter main courses. The traditional version calls for expensive porcini mushrooms, but where I grew up in Sicily, we didn't have easy access to them, so my mum loved to make this dish with cheaper, easier-to-find oyster mushrooms. Here the delicate flavor of the oyster mushrooms is jazzed up by a few simple ingredients to make a super tasty, quick and inexpensive side for any occasion.

Serves 4

2 lb (900 g) oyster mushrooms

¼ cup (60 ml) extra-virgin olive oil

1 clove garlic, lightly crushed

Sea salt and freshly cracked black pepper

1 tbsp (15 g) butter

2 tbsp (5 g) fresh parsley leaves, finely minced

Rinse the mushrooms quickly under cool running water, then pat them dry. Cut them into strips if they're very large, or keep them whole if they're small.

Heat the extra-virgin olive oil in a large pan over medium-low heat. Add the garlic and cook until it begins to turn golden brown. Discard the garlic, and add the mushrooms to the pan.

Sauté the mushrooms for 5 minutes over medium-high heat, or until cooked through. Then season with sea salt and black pepper to taste.

Remove the pan from the heat, and stir in the butter. Top the mushrooms with fresh parsley, stir gently and serve immediately.

Tip: *This basic recipe works great with any kind of mushrooms. My favorite varieties to use, aside from oyster, are porcini, shiitake and chanterelle mushrooms.*

Garlicky Stir-Fried Broccoli

 Gluten-Free, Vegan

Super nutritious and versatile, this garlicky stir-fried broccoli is my go-to side on a busy weeknight. It's loaded with flavor and goes well with pretty much anything, from meat to poultry to fish to fried eggs. The almonds add a sweet note and a lovely crunchiness, and if you can handle the heat, feel free to sprinkle your broccoli with chili flakes for a nice spicy kick.

Serves 4

4 cups (350 g) broccoli florets, halved

3 tbsp (45 ml) extra-virgin olive oil

1 clove garlic, grated

Juice and zest of ½ lemon

Sea salt and freshly cracked black pepper

⅔ cup (60 g) toasted almond flakes, for garnish

Bring a large pot of lightly salted water to a boil, then drop in the broccoli florets and cook for 4 to 5 minutes, or until tender.

With the help of a slotted spoon, transfer the florets to a bowl with cold water and ice. Then drain and set aside.

Heat the extra-virgin olive oil in a large pan over medium heat. Add the broccoli and garlic, and stir-fry them for 2 minutes. Drizzle the broccoli with lemon juice, sprinkle with lemon zest and season with sea salt and black pepper to taste.

Transfer the broccoli to a serving plate, and top with toasted almonds.

Tip: *This recipe works well with most vegetables. If you're looking for a different vegetable to replace the broccoli, my favorites include green beans, potatoes, asparagus and cauliflower.*

Sautéed Purple Potatoes & Romanesco Broccoli

🌾 Gluten-Free

Purple potatoes and Romanesco broccoli have recently gained more popularity internationally, but they're steeped in Italian cooking tradition. For a quick side, I like to sauté them together and give them a kick of flavor by drizzling a velvety, umami-packed Parmesan sauce all over them. This luxurious cheese sauce is perfect to elevate even the simplest veggies such as potatoes and broccoli, and you can use the leftovers to dress a big bowl of pasta the next day!

Serves 4

1 lb (450 g) small purple potatoes, peeled and cut into 1-inch (2½-cm) cubes

3⅓ cups (300 g) Romanesco broccoli, cut into small florets

3½ oz (100 g) Parmesan cheese, finely grated

3 fl oz (100 ml) fresh heavy cream

A pinch of freshly grated nutmeg

Sea salt and freshly cracked black pepper

2 tbsp (30 ml) good-quality extra-virgin olive oil

½ medium yellow onion, thinly sliced

1 medium carrot, peeled and cut into thin slices diagonally

Bring a pot of lightly salted water to a boil. Drop the potatoes into the boiling water and cook for about 10 minutes. Halfway through the cooking time, add the Romanesco broccoli and continue to cook until the vegetables are tender.

Place the Parmesan cheese and heavy cream in a small pot and cook, stirring occasionally, over low heat, until the sauce reaches a creamy velvety consistency, about 3 to 4 minutes. Season with a pinch of nutmeg and sea salt and black pepper to taste. Set the sauce aside until needed.

Heat the extra-virgin olive oil in a large frying pan. Add the onion and carrot, and sauté for a couple of minutes. Drain the potatoes and Romanesco broccoli, transfer them to the pan and sauté all the ingredients for 1 to 2 minutes. Season with sea salt and black pepper to taste, and remove the pan from the heat.

Transfer the vegetables to a large serving plate, and drizzle with the desired quantity of Parmesan sauce.

Tip: *Purple potatoes have a slightly nutty flavor similar to chestnuts and work amazingly well in this recipe. If you can't find them, substitute with tiny Italian new potatoes—there's no need to peel them.*

Super-Fast Stir-Fried Aromatic Fennel

 Vegan

The refreshing licorice-like flavor of fennel comes out at its best in this simple side dish. Deeply aromatic and super-fast to prepare, this stir-fried fennel makes a great side to pair with both meat and fish courses over the winter season.

Serves 4

2 tbsp (30 ml) extra-virgin olive oil

3 fennel bulbs, sliced

1 small white onion, finely sliced

1 tbsp (8 g) panko breadcrumbs

½ tbsp (1 g) freshly dried Italian oregano

Sea salt and freshly cracked pink pepper

Heat the extra-virgin olive oil in a large pan over medium-high heat.

Toss in the fennel and onion, and stir-fry them for 2 minutes.

Cover the pan with a lid and continue to cook over low heat for 5 minutes, or until the fennel is just tender. Return the heat to medium-high. Sprinkle the panko breadcrumbs and oregano over the fennel, and stir-fry for 1 minute. Season with sea salt and pink peppercorns to taste.

Sautéed Brussels Sprouts with Crispy Pancetta

 Dairy-Free, Gluten-Free

Crunchy sautéed Brussels sprouts are brightened up with fresh lemon juice and finished off with toasted walnuts and classic Italian pancetta in this tasty side dish. This is definitely my favorite way to cook Brussels sprouts. It's a veggie my family didn't eat too often when I was growing up, but I've learned to love it during my adult years in the U.K. I especially love to make these sautéed Brussels sprouts with pancetta for festive dinner parties because they're speedy, delicious and always get amazing reviews!

Serves 4

12 oz (350 g) Brussels sprouts, cleaned and halved

3 tbsp (45 ml) extra-virgin olive oil

3½ oz (100 g) pancetta, cubed

½ cup (60 g) walnuts, chopped

Zest of ½ lemon

Sea salt and freshly cracked black pepper

Bring a large pot of lightly salted water to a boil, then drop in the Brussels sprouts and cook for 5 to 7 minutes, or until just tender.

With the help of a slotted spoon, transfer the Brussels sprouts to a bowl with cold water and ice. Drain and set them aside.

Heat the extra-virgin olive oil in a large pan over medium heat. Add the Brussels sprouts and pancetta, and sauté for 2 minutes, or until the pancetta is crispy. Fold in the walnuts, sprinkle with the lemon zest and season with sea salt and black pepper to taste. Transfer the Brussels sprouts to a serving plate.

Tip: *I like to add nuts for an extra nutritious touch and a bit of lemon zest to freshen up the veggies. Feel free to leave these ingredients out to keep it more traditional.*

Acknowledgments

To my dear Papino, you were and will always be my biggest fan. You made me feel special and loved. I'm sure that you'd be so proud of me and this cookbook. There are no words to describe how much I love you.

To Mum, you're the strongest person I know. Thank you for teaching me to be just as strong. Without you and your infinite love for food and cooking, this book would have never been possible.

To Valerio, thank you for your infinite love, patience and support over the years. You're the best taster, recipe reviewer, photography assistant, hand model and above all, the best dad and partner I could ever dream of. I'm honored to have you in my life.

To Noah, you're simply the most gorgeous and delightful baby I know. You have helped me around the kitchen in your own unique way. Your love, laughs and you just being you make my life infinitely better, and I'm proud to be your mamma.

To Emiliano, Luca, Matteo e Luna. Guys, you're the most incredible brothers and sister I could ask for. Your infinite support over the years and during my time writing this cookbook cheered me up, fueled me and kept me going.

To Umberto, thank you for sticking by my side for most of my life. Our time together made me the person I am today. You helped me and believed in me in so many ways that an entire acknowledgments page wouldn't be enough to list them. Most of all, you made The Petite Cook possible, and I'll be forever grateful for that.

To my dear friend Elena, you've always believed in me and offered me my first-ever job. You pushed me into a creative cooking stream that made me hungry for more and made me realize this was the career I wanted to pursue. You also persuaded me to create The Petite Cook blog, and for that, I'll never thank you enough.

To Mauro, for teaching me how to make gnocchi. It was one of my earliest cooking classes ever, and I will never forget it. I probably never told you that it made me fall in love with cooking even more.

To Jenna, you are the best editor I could ask for. You have been absolutely crucial to making this cookbook possible. Your endless work, support and precious advice helped me put into words my memories, cooking experiments and concepts, and ultimately helped me draft a cookbook I'm really proud of.

To the whole amazing team behind Page Street Publishing, you have believed in me and in my cookbook concept from the very first moment, and for this I will never thank you enough.

About the Author

Andrea is the founder, recipe developer and photographer of the popular blog The Petite Cook. What began as a place to chronicle her foodie experiments is now one of the top U.K. food blogs with millions of readers coming to her site, and over 700,000 followers on social media hungry for quick Italian-inspired weeknight recipes and other modern dishes inspired by her travels around the world.

Her recipes have been featured on numerous websites and magazines, including *The Guardian, Parade, Country Living, Elle* and *Great British Chefs*, and she traveled to Japan with CNN to discover the most remote restaurant in Kyoto. Before starting her blog, Andrea worked in numerous top Michelin-starred restaurants and was the marketing manager of a popular recipe app. She now divides her time between London and a small rural town in Germany, where she continues to cook and write along with her partner and their gorgeous baby son, Noah. Visit her at thepetitecook.com for more cooking inspiration.

Index